**Public Administration
Education in Transition**

ANNALS OF PUBLIC ADMINISTRATION

Editor-in-Chief

JACK RABIN

Rider College
Lawrenceville, New Jersey

MARGARET ROSE, Assistant to the Editor-in-Chief

Managing Editors

GERALD J. MILLER   W. BARTLEY HILDRETH

University of Kansas   Kent State University
Lawrence, Kansas   Kent, Ohio

Topic Areas

A complete listing of editors' affiliations and editorial boards can be found at the end of this volume.

Bureaucracy / Jack Rabin, Editor
Criminal Justice Administration / William A. Jones, Jr., Editor
Health and Human Resources Administration / Robert Agranoff, Editor
Implementation / Frank Thompson, Editor
Intergovernmental Relations / Richard H. Leach, Editor
Organization Management / Chester A. Newland, Editor
Policy Formulation and Evaluation / G. Ronald Gilbert, Editor
Public Administration Education / Thomas Vocino, Editor
Public Administration History and Theory / Joseph A. Uveges, Jr., Editor
Public Budgeting and Financial Management / Thomas Lynch, Editor
Public Personnel Administration and Labor Relations / David H. Rosenbloom, Editor
Regulation and Administrative Law / Victor Rosenblum, Editor
Research Methods in Public Administration / Frank P. Scioli, Jr., Editor

Volume 1. Public Administration: History and Theory in Contemporary Perspective, edited by Joseph A. Uveges, Jr.
Volume 2. Public Administration Education in Transition, edited by Thomas Vocino and Richard Heimovics
Volume 3. Centenary Issues of the Pendleton Act of 1883, edited by David H. Rosenbloom with the assistance of Mark A. Emmert

(other volumes in preparation)

Public Administration Education in Transition

edited by

THOMAS VOCINO
Auburn University at Montgomery
Montgomery, Alabama

RICHARD HEIMOVICS
University of Missouri - Kansas City
Kansas City, Missouri

MARCEL DEKKER, INC.   New York and Basel

Library of Congress Cataloging in Publication Data
Main entry under title:

Public administration education in transition.

(Annals of public administration, ISSN 0278-
4289 ; v. 2)
Includes index.
1. Public administration—Study and teaching—
United States—Addresses, essays, lectures.
2. Public administration—United States—Addresses,
essays, lectures. I. Vocino, Thomas. II. Heimovics,
Richard, [date] . III. Series.
JF1338.A2P824   1982   350'.0007'073   82-9975
ISBN 0-8247-1674-4   AACR2

MARCEL DEKKER, INC.
270 Madison Avenue, New York, New York 10016

Current printing (last digit):
10 9 8 7 6 5 4 3 2 1

Printed in the United States of America

About the Series

The Annals of Public Administration is designed to present issues of topical concern to the public administration community. The series brings together the efforts of several hundred scholars and practitioners in thirteen topic areas of public administration.

The goal of the Annals, therefore, is to encourage the most widespread dissemination of ideas. All volumes will be the product of the interaction between a topic-area editor for each topic area and a group of experts serving as both editorial board and as advisors.

The topic areas to be covered in the Annals are:

1. Bureaucracy
2. Criminal Justice Administration
3. Health and Human Resources Administration
4. Implementation
5. Intergovernmental Relations
6. Organization Management
7. Policy Formulation and Evaluation
8. Public Administration Education
9. Public Administration History and Theory
10. Public Budgeting and Financial Management
11. Public Personnel Administration and Labor Relations
12. Regulation and Administrative Law
13. Research Methods in Public Administration

Because the series tries to remain up to date on current issues and topics in the field, it is quite important for the editor-in-chief and the topic-area editors to receive feedback from readers. What is your evaluation of the ways in which authors have approached the issues covered in a particular volume? What topics do you foresee will become important issues for the profession in the future? Please address your remarks to the topic-area editor and/or editor-in-chief.

We hope that the *Annals of Public Administration* will fulfill its goal and become a useful tool for the public administration community.

Jack Rabin

Preface

The purpose of *Public Administration Education* is to introduce its readers to
some of the major issues facing public administration education in the 1980s.
Its central theme is the challenge of improving the quality of education for
the public service. The decade of the 1970s saw the establishment of many
new, and the expansion of older, public service education programs. For the
field of public administration, the 1980s will also see, in our view, a growth
in some programs; however, the decade as described in the following chapters
will be one in which evaluation of public administration education will
probably be more prominent than it was in the 1970s. This concern with
quality is reflected in the implementation of the Peer Review process (quasi-
accreditation) of the National Association of Schools of Public Affairs and
Administration for master's-level programs. Peer Review is only the beginning of an effort to impose higher standards in the delivery of public
administration education.

A major issue for discussion in the coming decade is that of doctoral
education. It seems almost a certainty that an area for expansion in the
1980s will be the doctoral offerings in public administration, especially
those programs designed to enhance the credentials of practitioners. Furthermore, some of the new models for the delivery of doctoral education in
public administration are the subject of controversy in the field. In the
opening chapter of this volume, William Earle Klay indicates several problems
with the most prominent of the innovators in doctoral education, Nova

University. Klay's critique of Nova relates to a number of factors, including Nova's lack of resident centers with resident faculty, one week of full-time study a year on the main Nova campus, and the lack of a local library. These and other factors are major obstacles to offering a doctoral program of high quality. As Professor Klay's comments tend to represent traditional perspectives of the academic community, we asked Ralph Chandler to add another perspective on nontraditional doctoral education. Professor Chandler argues that programs similar to Nova's can be rigorous if implemented properly and that the graduates of these programs can legitimately claim to have earned a quality doctorate. Whether one is oriented toward traditional or nontraditional approaches to doctoral education, the essays of Professors Klay and Chandler offer administrators, instructors, and students considerable "food for thought."

The number of women enrolled in public administration programs has grown significantly in the last decade, as has been the case for many other professionally oriented university programs. Naomi B. Lynn deals with the emerging issues related to the education of women for the public service. Generally, she explores ways of making public administration education more meaningful for the female student, and, more specifically, it is her contention from an examination of a number of public administration textbooks that inadequate attention is paid to women in public organizations, a problem that needs rectification. In sum, Lynn sees important differences between the sexes in their role as public managers and argues that public administration education should recognize these differences and develop approaches to education based on them.

James S. Bowman and Jeremy F. Plant address the issue of the proper role of ethics education in the public administration curriculum. Basically, they argue that public administration faculty should assist in the development of a value orientation for students. Without a sense of purpose (as well as the analytical skills developed in a public administration program), the graduates of these programs, Bowman and Plant argue, will be less capable of having a positive impact on their organizations. Bowman and Plant also discuss the effect that structural arrangements for public administration programs may have on the values of students.

A major clientele of public administration programs in the 1970s has been the in-service, adult student. It seems that this group will continue to constitute a major proportion of the students in public administration education programs in the 1980s. Two chapters in this volume attempt to address the issue of how public administration programs can most effectively foster learning for the in-service, adult student. Deborah J. Young and

William B. Eddy explore the literature on adult education for ideas of how public administration education can begin to meet the needs of this clientele. They also explore in a comprehensive fashion the innovative approaches to adult education that many public administration programs currently have in use. Richard Skruber and Ann-Marie Rizzo discuss critical issues in the design of a "democratic framework" for teaching the adult learner. They argue that the motivational level of these students increases when they play an important role in the development of the educational experience and recommend that the adult learners become "co-producers" of their educational program.

The proper role of theory in public administration programs has long been debated. Guy B. Adams asserts that the organizational theory taught in most public administration programs is inadequate. More specifically, he argues that the theories borrowed from other disciplines in the social sciences are ineffective in educating individuals for the public service. Professor Adams examines the epistomological limitations of theories currently being taught and offers suggestions for the development of more relevant theories for the public administration education curriculum.

The final chapter of this volume examines the career paths and opportunities for public administration educators. Specifically, James F. Wolf reviews the trends in career development, indicates how careers in public administration can be enhanced while an individual serves in academic and practitioner environments, and offers perspectives on the advantages and disadvantages of various career paths for those earning the doctorate in public administration.

Finally, we would like to acknowledge that this volume benefited greatly from the thoughtful comments of the Editorial Board of the Public Administration Education Section of the *Annals of Public Administration*. The Editorial Board members are: Yong H. Cho, University of Akron; Leigh Grosenick, Virginia Commonwealth University; James T. Jones, Atlanta University; John E. Kerrigan, University of Nebraska, Omaha; James D. Kitchen, San Diego State University; Elliott H. Kline, University of the Pacific; Herman Mertins, Jr., West Virginia University; Jerome M. Mileur, University of Massachusetts; Charldean Newell, North Texas State University; Mel D. Powell, California State University, Long Beach; and Orba F. Traylor (Professor Emeritus), University of Alabama, Huntsville.

Thomas Vocino
Richard Heimovics

Contributors

Guy B. Adams Graduate Program in Public Administration, Evergreen State College, Olympia, Washington

James S. Bowman Department of Public Administration, Florida State University, Tallahassee, Florida

Ralph Clark Chandler Department of Political Science and Center for Public Administration Programs, Western Michigan University, Kalamazoo, Michigan

William B. Eddy Department of Public Administration, University of Missouri, Kansas City, Missouri

William Earle Klay Department of Public Administration, Florida State University, Tallahassee, Florida

Naomi B. Lynn Department of Political Science, Kansas State University, Manhattan, Kansas

Jeremy F. Plant Department of Public Affairs, George Mason University, Fairfax, Virginia

Ann-Marie Rizzo Department of Public Administration, Florida International University, North Miami, Florida

Richard Skruber   Department of Public Administration, Florida International University, North Miami, Florida

James F. Wolf   Center for Public Administration and Policy, Virginia Polytechnic Institute and State University, Falls Church, Virginia

Deborah J. Young*   Department of Public Administration, University of Missouri, Kansas City, Missouri

*Present affiliation: Training and Career Development, General Services Administration, Kansas City, Missouri

Contents

**Public Administration
Education in Transition**

1

Innovations and Standards in Public Administration Education

William Earle Klay
Florida State University, Tallahassee, Florida

The burgeoning of public administration programs during the past decade presents our interdiscipline/profession with a new set of challenges. Our educational services are now being delivered to more persons than ever before, but questions are being raised as to whether such growth is being achieved at the expense of quality.[1,2] The rapid growth which has taken place is the result of much innovation in the teaching and scheduling of classes. The extent of this innovation is evident from the fact that the typical graduate student in public administration is now an in-service person pursuing a degree on a part-time basis, often at locations removed from college campuses.

· Public administration education has evidenced an ethos of advocacy and equity in that programs have been designed to overcome barriers to persons who stand to benefit from our services and who otherwise would be denied them. The result of this growth and innovation, however, is a sharp departure of professional education in public administration from the traditional norms of both academic and professional schools, which have emphasized lengthy periods of full-time residence. Public administration is now relatively unique among the fields of professional education in that not only primary professional studies, but doctoral programs as well, are widely available through nontraditional modes. This uniqueness imposes certain obligations on us to carefully study what we are doing and to ensure that the pursuit of equity has not been at the expense of quality.

An Extensive Commitment to the Nontraditional

Enrollment data submitted by member institutions of the National Association of Schools of Public Affairs and Administration (NASPAA) for the 1978–1979 academic year are indicative of the extent to which public administration has departed from the traditional. These reveal that 64 percent of all graduate students were studying on a part-time basis and that in 112 programs a majority of students were part-time attendees. Furthermore, some 27 percent of all graduate students were reported as being enrolled in off-campus programs offered by 59 member institutions. This is an understatement of actual off-campus activity, however, because some institutions with class offerings at locations away from main campuses, but within metropolitan commuting distances, did not report such off-campus enrollments.

Because they represent the sharpest departures from traditional modes, off-campus programs are of special importance and concern. Off-campus education is now popular even at the doctoral level, with some institutions such as Southern California and Virginia Tech having established residence centers where doctorates may be earned at locations far removed from the main campuses. Of particular concern for doctoral education, however, is the fact that at least one regionally accredited NASPAA member is now offering doctorates at numerous off-campus locations throughout the nation without establishing permanent instructional centers. As Table 1 indicates, Nova University, an institution which relies heavily upon part-time faculty to offer its instructional services, awarded 59 percent of all DPA degrees nationally in 1979 and 31 percent of all doctorates (Ph. D. and DPA combined) in that same year.

Many off-campus programs use evening classes which are only slight modifications of the traditional day courses that meet throughout a quarter or semester. Those programs which are more distant from main campuses, however, tend to rely more upon variations of the "intensive seminar" format. The University of Oklahoma, which offers its MPA degree at locations around the world, for example, assigns readings to students several weeks in advance

Table 1 Doctorates Awarded in 1975 and 1979 by
All Institutions and by Nova University

	Year	
	1975	1979
Ph.D. (All institutions)	82	94
DPA (Other institutions)	39	43
DPA (Nova)	0	62
Total (All institutions)	121	199

Source: Data from NASPAA, *Programs in Public Affairs
and Administration*, NASPAA, Washington, D.C., 1978
and 1980 editions.

of a course session and then arranges for faculty to meet with students for 30
classroom hours in no more than 10 days. Similarly, personal contact between students and faculty members in the Nova University DPA program is
accomplished through 18 weekend seminars and 3 week-long seminars.

It is unfortunate, but necessary, that public administration must now face
the possibility that its extensive commitment to off-campus education may
bring it increasingly unfavorable attention. The controversy and turmoil
regarding off-campus programs for teachers and school administrators which
is now growing in the education profession may be a precursor of what is to
come in public administration. Sharp criticism and rebuttals regarding the
quality of external doctoral programs in education are becoming increasingly
common in that discipline's professional journals and in various newspapers
as well (see *Phi Delta Kappan*, November 1978 and April 1979 for a series of
articles on the topic).[3,4] Of greatest concern is the fact that the primary
focus of this controversy is the Ed.D. program of Nova University. This
program is essentially similar to that institution's DPA program, which is also
becoming a center of controversy.[5,6]

Competitiveness between public administration programs has increased as
a consequence of the growth and nontraditional emphasis that has occurred.
Furthermore, it is self-delusion to presume that institutional competitiveness
is not a motivating factor in the development of programs. A discussion of
the recent development of a DPA program, for example, revealed that it was
started partly because a rival state institution had begun offering a new
doctorate at a nearby residence center.[7] Competition can be a constructive

force in some situations, but it can also contribute to a diminution of quality and rigor. Such competition can create pressures to lessen the requirements applied to a given credential, or to offer a higher credential such as a DPA rather than the MPA, without requiring a corresponding increase in level of effort and accomplishment.

The negative aspects of entrepreneurially oriented competition in higher education have been well identified.[8] I have had the misfortune of personally observing such undesirable competition between MPA programs on a military base, a setting in which an absence of sufficient concern for quality is apparently not uncommon.[9] In response to a request from a military base for an MPA program, I suggested a program in which classroom instruction would be on base, but in which students would have to occasionally commute a distance of some 80 miles to a main campus to utilize the university's library on weekends, as well as to participate in occasional on-campus visits from visiting scholars and administrators. The base commander and educational officer responded that they could obtain MPA programs from other institutions which would require no such participation or access to libraries. Whether this was an isolated incident or symptomatic of a larger pattern, it is clear that the extensive use of nontraditional instructional modes in public administration obligates our profession to become more sensitive to the dynamics and possible effects of institutional competition.

The Equivalency Question

Perhaps the greatest question associated with nontraditional innovations in education is that of equivalency. To some degree this question is addressed in the NASPAA standards. Masters degree Standard 9.1, for example, states that ". . . off-campus programs require special planning and control in order to insure that they are offered under the same quality standards as maintained at the parent campus."[10] This same standard places the responsibility for demonstrating equivalency upon those who develop and offer the innovations. Requiring innovators to shoulder the burden of proof for equivalency is a pattern which has been generally accepted in higher education, but charges that traditional modes are essentially elitist have been made on various occasions, and such accusations tend to shift the burden to the traditionalists.

In this context, it is notable that the University of Oklahoma, one of the pioneers in off-campus education for public administration, has used the equivalency criterion for its own evaluation of the intensive seminar mode of instruction.[11] An equivalency analysis was attempted in two ways: first, through comparison of test scores and survey responses from 21 graduates of Oklahoma's regular program with those of 181 off-campus program graduates. Second, responses of 12 visiting faculty members were compared to the responses of 21 regular faculty members. Both faculty groups were experienced with traditional teaching as well as the intensive seminar mode. In most categories chosen for the faculty members to compare—amount of material assigned and covered, preparation of students, and encouragement of discussion—the responses suggested perceived equivalence. Most faculty members, however (64 percent) stated that the inability to assign term papers was a detraction, and some said that this was a major weakness which results in "poorer quality final research papers."[12]

Surveys of students enrolled in off-campus programs seem to indicate general satisfaction with the instruction received. Studies done by Oklahoma, the University of San Francisco,[13] and by Nova University for its DPA program[14] show similar positive response patterns. Such surveys may be important measures for a variety of purposes; they are seriously lacking, however, as measures of equivalency. Students in the off-campus programs, for example, lack a frame of reference in traditional public administration programs of an equivalent degree level to use as a basis for comparison.

In its preoccupation with growth, the public administration community has concerned itself with program inputs to the neglect of output measurements. This is especially evident in the NASPAA standards which are focused primarily upon inputs. These standards are comparable to those used in other fields of education. Their enforcement, however, will not stimulate the creation of the knowledge which is necessary to evaluate the effects of such innovations as off-campus intensive seminars, evening programs, and the like. Simply stated, input-oriented standards generate input-oriented self-study processes.

The evaluative research which is needed to study program outputs—the learning of facts, skills, and values—faces a variety of methodological obstacles. First, to ensure that impartiality prevails, research should be directed by persons who are not personally involved in promoting the instructional modes that are being evaluated. Perhaps NASPAA could assemble a roster of educational evaluators who would be willing to perform such research for other institutions in return for expenses and purchased release time rather than personal consultant fees. Second, to ensure that sufficient persons are involved as members of both experimental and control groups, it may be necessary to study the programs of several institutions simultaneously. Great care must be taken to ensure that experimental and control groups are comparable in terms of experience and other predictors of graduate performance.

   Third, it is likely that instruments for the measurement of outputs will
have to be specially designed. The Oklahoma evaluation[15] admirably tried to
construct an output measure from final comprehensive examinations but
found this to be quite difficult because each faculty member had used his or
her own peculiar grading system. The results showed that students in the
traditional program performed somewhat better on the examinations but
these findings are inconclusive due to the small number of students involved
in the traditional mode and an absence of controls regarding differences in
the time elapsed between matriculation and graduation for the two groups.
Specially developed tests, employer surveys, and graded simulations are
possible evaluation instruments which may be useful as output measures.
Such research will require major investments of resources, but the extensive
commitment of public administration to nontraditional education obligates
us to do so.

The Coming Technological Revolution

The same commitment also obligates us to explore new ways of overcoming
those weaknesses which we now perceive. One such weakness, as the Oklahoma evaluation reveals, is associated with the immobility of libraries and
computer facilities. In this regard, many of the logistical obstacles to off-
campus education may cease to exist if full advantage is taken of the revolution in computer and communications technology that is now taking place.
   Though libraries are by no means the only source of important information for public administration students, they are indisputably valuable repos-
itories of human knowledge and experience. They assume special importance
as places where our students can pursue their own intellectual interests, and
any educational program, professionally oriented or otherwise, which isolates
students from this source seems dangerously close to becoming depersonal-
ized, "canned" training. The importance of libraries is underscored in
NASPAA standards with doctoral Standard 2.4 calling for "systematic access
to appropriate library and data resources," and master's Standard 9.5 emphasizing that "students in off-campus programs should have reasonable access
to a graduate level collection . . . , computer facilities, and other appropriate
academic support services."[16]
   Microtechnology is now being applied to libraries with amazing results.
Some on-line, full-text information retrieval services already exist, and
society should eventually see a time when the Library of Congress becomes a
publicly accessible data base.[17,18] Even relatively small public libraries are

now installing terminals which can be linked to full-text central data sources, as well as on-line printers. One of the distinguishing features of this new technology is that it essentially eliminates geographical barriers to obtaining information. Public administration has substantially committed itself to the widely decentralized delivery of its educational services. Our profession, therefore, should move rapidly to make the fullest possible use of an emerging technology which lends itself so well to such decentralization.

NASPAA, the American Society for Public Administration, and the National Academy of Public Administration should seek support from a variety of sources, such as the National Science Foundation, to begin an effort to place much of the literature of public administration into an on-line retrieval system. Such a project would become more feasible if various member institutions would pool their efforts and resources. Once an administrative and fee-sharing structure for the project is established, the project could begin by identifying a dozen or so journals and perhaps a hundred or so books for initial inclusion.

Other aspects of the emerging electronic technology also hold promise for enhancing public administration education, both on and off campus. Wider use of audio or video tapes, for example, will allow the instructors of intensive seminar type courses to present introductory lectures and research assignments to students several weeks or months prior to the seminar meetings. A development which holds especially great promise is teleconferencing, the use of two-way video interaction, or of one-way video with telephonic feedback. Cooperative participation in this new technique will allow groups of students and administrators at points around the nation, or globe, to hear the profession's most distinguished scholars and practitioners through a medium which allows interaction. The cost-effectiveness of such a conference system is improving rapidly when compared with the growing energy costs of travel.

Computer-assisted instruction is also reaching a stage of considerable sophistication. Although public administration has made relatively little use of this mode of instruction, there is much in our curriculum which lends itself to it. The conveyance of technical knowledge and skills is especially amenable to computer assistance: statistics, governmental accounting, cash flow and investment analysis, elements of position analysis and classification, and similar topics are promising in this regard. Of particular interest is the ability of the newer computer techniques to engage students in simulations, and it seems likely that the administrator of the future will need to be competent with such interactive decision techniques.[19]

The Unanswered Question of Personal Contact
and Professional Socialization

It may well be, then, that extensive use of computer-based technology will
remove most of the logistical barriers of access to information which have
heretofore confounded off-campus programs. If public administration moves
to utilize this technology, however, it can then expect to be confronted more
than ever before by another equally important problem—namely, the importance of personal contact between professor and student. The importance of
this contact has been challenged by external degree programs which have
greatly reduced the potential for informal face-to-face contact. We know
very little about the quality, or even quantity, of personal contact in the
traditional full-time mode, and even less about the nontraditional ones to
which our profession is now heavily committed.

Public administrators exercise influence and authority—they do unto
others. Education for public administration, therefore, cannot be content
merely to convey science; it must also be concerned with how knowledge
and power are used. Dwight Waldo, for example, has stressed that we should
not think of ourselves so much as an academic discipline but rather think
"that the paradigm that is most important is an overarching professional
paradigm."[20] One of the distinguishing characteristics of those occupational
groups which are most readily defined as professions is the existence of certain standards of behavior that are somehow conveyed from generation to
generation.

The National Academy of Public Administration's influential report on
education stated in 1973 that the conveyance of "an underlying ethos of
public service" was a "critical need" in the education of public administrators.[21] It is interesting, however, that in the NASPAA standards which were
subsequently developed, more explicit attention was given to the socializing
role of faculty in the doctoral guidelines and standards than in the master's
standards. Doctoral Guideline 3.2, applicable to both Ph.D. and DPA programs, states, "The faculty serves as role models from which students may
draw some of their values, behavior, and skill cues as researchers, practitioners, and teachers."[22]

In addition to the vital question as to what the normative dimensions of
such an ethos should be, the educators of our profession must know more
about the quality, intensity, and duration of interaction which is necessary
to convey it. In this regard, public administration must confess to profound
ignorance. Much has been written in the sociological literature about socialization, but relatively little has been done regarding the socializing effect of

higher education upon managerial students, especially public ones. Comparative studies of the socialization patterns in traditional full-time, part-time, and off-campus programs are much needed. A recent survey of MPA students from nine southeastern universities may be indicative of differences which are now occurring. This survey found that 47.5 percent of full-time students belonged to professional organizations while only 16.7 percent of their part-time counterparts were members of such organizations.[23]

Off-campus education is directed primarily to persons who are public employees and who have, therefore, already undergone presumably extensive socialization experiences in public organizations. If the ethos of public service as perceived by faculty members is essentially congruent with that which is conveyed within these organizations, then the question of socialization experiences for mid-career persons is essentially irrelevant. In such a circumstance, off-campus education need only be concerned with imparting basic knowledge and skills. If the educators in our profession, however, wish to instill values different from those that prevail within the socialization experiences in public organizations, the question of socialization becomes a critical one.

Replication and expansion of a study design applied by Edgar Schein to business education over a decade ago would be especially helpful in coming to grips with the socialization question.[24] The attitudes of four separate groups were identified and compared: those of a small group of senior executives who attended a short course together, inexperienced regular master's students, mid-career master's students who were in a twelve month residency program, and the faculty of the program. Although there was heterogeneity among the faculty, particularly as a function of teaching area, it was observed that, on at least half of the scales, the faculty tended to differ from the attitudes of the senior executives. The initial attitudes of both student groups were intermediate, and it was observed that the attitudes of both groups exhibited a clear trend toward the adoption of faculty attitudes. Both groups generally became " . . . less accepting of classical management principles, less conservative, more accepting of change and career movement, more trusting of workers, more accepting of group initiatives and decision making, and more interpersonally oriented."[25] Whether a similar effect can occur through off-campus programs, or even in part-time studies in traditional programs, is unknown.

The socialization question presents dilemmas. The nature of socializing experiences probably varies within and between education programs, just as it may vary within and between organizations. Criticisms may be expected from public officials where it is found that faculty hold attitudes different from their own, while criticisms will come from other sources if the attitudes of the two groups are found to be congruent.[26]   It may well be, then, that the best hope for a consensus approach to the socialization question is to take greater care to observe the manner in which we educators deliver the public service with which we are entrusted—education. Denhardt has argued, for example, that socialization in public administration programs occurs primarily through the manner in which educational services are organized and delivered.[27] No groups should take exception to a socialization process which attempts to instill values of quality and individualized service by example.

An Agenda for Research and Action

Although public administration must do much more to learn about program outputs, it may be advisable not to adopt standards which are explicitly output oriented. Such output measures, as in the case of standardized examinations, could result in teaching "to the test," rather than stimulating continuing efforts to keep curricula abreast of changing times. From the perspectives of creativity, responsiveness, and academic freedom, it may be wiser to continue to stress standards of a logistical sort such as those regarding sufficient faculty and resources. Output-oriented studies are badly needed, however, to better inform the collective judgment of the profession as to what constitutes appropriate inputs.

Unfortunately, the profession must quickly face the possibility that its reputation is suffering due to ambiguities that now exist in NASPAA standards and guidelines for doctoral programs. These standards may have to be reconsidered and applied for accreditation type purposes before major output evaluations can be done. For example, the doctoral guidelines and standards call for an "appropriate environment" with "program facilities" and "facilities for informal contact," for "close, continuous working relationships between doctoral students and appropriate faculty," and for "systematic access to appropriate library and data resources," among other things.[28]

The criteria imply that an acceptable doctoral education can only be taught through a well-supported residence center in a community, but nowhere is this explicitly stated as such. Similarly, the minutes of the April, 1975 meeting at which the doctoral guidelines were adopted by NASPAA indicate that a strong consensus existed regarding the importance of full time study, but no minimum period was stated. Consequently, the institution which now awards more doctorates than any other and which claims to be in full conformance, does so without establishing centers with resident faculty, local library, or other facilities, and which requires only one week of full-time study each year in a single curriculum which is totally standardized for all students.

Public administration can establish an accreditation or "conformance" process to encourage the highest possible quality in doctoral education without unduly restricting innovations that depart sharply from traditional modes. Placement on a list of accredited or conforming doctoral institutions should be restricted to programs taught through main campus or residence centers, but with a temporary applicant status for external degree programs which lack major residence center facilities. This applicant status could be converted to full acceptance, and the standards themselves might be changed, if the petitioning innovators present acceptable evidence of equivalence gained from truly rigorous and objective output-oriented research. Such research would be required to conform to methodological guidelines and equivalency standards established by NASPAA. A similar process for petitioning and standards review in light of new research findings could also be applied to the current master's review process.

The day may come when external programs that fully utilize the new information technology, and which pay close attention to the quality of personal interaction, will become equivalent to more traditional programs. In the meantime, public administration must pursue two paths with equal vigor and resolve: first, to lead in the development of the new electronic technology, and second, to insure that students who receive recognized degrees in our profession will have done so only in an environment that instills a concern for quality and for individualized service to each person. Substandard or completely standardized mass production processes cannot be tolerated, for if such programs are offered, we may be preparing persons to deliver public services in a similar slipshod manner with no thought given to individual needs and differences.

Notes

1. Golembiewski, R. T. The Near-Future of Graduate Public Administration Programs in the U. S.: Some Program Minima, Their Common Violation, and Some Priority Palliatives. *Southern Review of Public Administration* *3*(3)(1979):323–359.
2. Downes, B. T. 1980's Public Management Issues/Challenges. *Proceedings of the Third National Conference on Teaching Public Administration*, Olympia, Wa., May 30–31, 1980, pp. 101–106.
3. Ashworth, K. H. The Nontraditional Doctorate: Time for *Sine Cera*? and Brown, R. G. The External Doctorate in Education: Growing Criticism and Crisis. *Phi Delta Kappan* *60*(3) (November 1978):173–176; 176–179.

4. Continuing the Debate on External Degrees: Symposium. *Phi Delta Kappan 60*(8) (May 1, 1980):559–574.
5. Georgia Rejects Nova Bid to Offer DPA Program. *PA Times 3*(9) (May 1, 1980):3, 8.
6. State Bans Doctorate from Nova. *Atlanta Journal,* April 10, 1980.
7. Plant, J. F. Designing a D.P.A. Core Seminar. *Proceedings of the Third National Conference on Teaching Public Administration,* Olympia, Wa., May 30–31, 1980, pp. 327–337.
8. Ashworth, K. *American Higher Education in Decline.* Texas A & M University Press, College Station, 1979.
9. Ashworth, K. H. and Lindley, W. C. The Disgrace of Military Base Programs. *Change: The Magazine of Higher Learning 9*(2)(1977):8.
10. *Standards for Professional Master's Degree Programs in Public Affairs/ Public Administration,* National Association of Schools of Public Affairs and Administration, Washington, D. C., 1977 (hereinafter cited as *Standards*).
11. Hebert, F. T. The Intensive Seminar Format: A Viable Scheduling Format. Revised from paper presented to Conference on the Teaching of Public Administration, Kansas City, Mo., May 5–6, 1978.
12. Ibid., p. 10.
13. Paige, D. Student Perceptions of Non-Traditional Public Administration Programs at U.S.F.. *Proceedings of the Third National Conference on Teaching Public Administration,* Olympia, Wa., May 30–31, 1980, pp. 321–326.
14. Nova University. The National DPA Program for Administrators: An Evaluation by Graduates, Center for Public Affairs and Administration, Fort Lauderdale, 1980.
15. Hebert, op. cit.
16. *Guidelines and Standards.* For Doctoral Degree Programs in Public Affairs/Public Administration, National Association of Schools of Public Affairs and Administration, Washington, D. C., 1976 (hereinafter cited as *Guidelines and Standards*), p. 2; *Standards,* p. 5.
17. 1985: New Technology for Libraries. *Library Journal* (July 1980): 1473–1478.
18. Roland, J. The Microelectronic Revolution. *The Futurist 3*(2)(1979): 81–90.
19. Simon, H. A. Applying Information Technology to Organization Design. *Public Administration Review 33*(3)(1973):268–278.
20. Waldo, D. Education for public administration in the seventies, in Mosher, F. C. (ed.), *American Public Administration: Past, Present, Future.* University of Alabama Press, University, Alabama, 1975, p. 224.
21. Chapman, R. L. and Cleaveland, F. N. *Meeting the Needs of Tomorrow's Public Service: Guidelines for Professional Education in Public Administration.* National Academy of Public Administration, Washington, D. C., 1973.
22. *Guidelines and Standards,* p. 3.

23. Ashmore, T., Lynch, S., and Threlkeld, S. P. A. Programs in the Southeast—An Alumni and Student Perspective. Paper presented to Southeastern Conference on Public Administration, Orlando, Florida, October 15–18, 1980.
24. Schein, E. H. Attitude Change during Management Education. *Administrative Science Quarterly 11*(1967):601–628.
25. Ibid., p. 617.
26. Yarwood, D. L. and Nimmo, D. D. Perspectives for Teaching Public Administration. *Midwest Review of Public Administration 9*(1)(1975): 28–42.
27. Denhardt, R. B. On the Management of Public Service Education. *Southern Review of Public Administration 3*(3)(1979):273–283.
28. *Guidelines and Standards,* p. 2.

2

A Few Kind Words for Nontraditional Education

Ralph Clark Chandler
Western Michigan University, Kalamazoo, Michigan

The author of the Chapter I have been asked to critique for the *Annals* (Chapter 1) is understandably concerned about the quality of nontraditional graduate education in public administration. The extensive commitment of the profession to nontraditional MPA and DPA programs raises questions about standards of all kinds, but specifically about equivalency, about our ability to utilize the revolution in computer and communications technology, and about the amount of personal contact between professor and student in noncampus settings. Underneath such concerns is the possibility that our professional reputation is suffering because of ambiguities existing in National Association of Schools of Public Affairs and Administration (NASPAA) standards and guidelines, and because some entrepreneurial enterprises such as Nova University take advantage of them.

All of these are legitimate concerns. But the author does not clarify what "quality" is, although he admits it is difficult to measure. Neither does he discriminate among a rather large number of nontraditional degree programs, some of which are more suspect than others. Finally, the role of the professor in the professional socialization of nontraditional graduate students is a matter of much more subtlety than we read here.

The following remarks are made, therefore, not to denigrate a thoughtful and challenging piece, but to help in the clarification of the distinctions I believe it is necessary to make to further our common goals.

A Distinction in Logic

The first distinction is merely a distinction in logic. The author appears to assume that quality is more likely to be present when the following conditions obtain: (1) The program is conducted on the main campus of a university. (2) The program requires a lengthy period of full-time residence. (3) The program has a substantial library nearby. (4) The program builds frequent personal contacts between professor and student. We are led to believe that when these conditions are not present, it might be appropriate to worry about the quality of the program.

Logically, if we could show even one instance of these four conditions being met, but resulting in a poor quality program, or a good quality program resulting from the neglect of *any* of these four conditions, the rest of the author's arguments would be inconsequential.

This is pedantic, of course, and unfair to the genuine considerations developed in the previous chapter. It does illustrate, however, the difficulty of the term *quality* and fundamental problems with the four categories themselves. Suppose one and two are absent, but three and four are present in a powerful way, as when microtechnology makes distant library information instantly retrieveable in a study center far from the main campus, and when a professor gives higher-quality time to off-campus than to on-campus students in his weekly exhilarating visits to reality.

The Need to Discriminate

The second distinction I wish to make is between Nova University and traditional universities which have devised innovative delivery systems for graduate education. Nova does indeed rely heavily on part-time, nonresident faculty and a single and totally standardized curriculum. In requiring only one week of full time study each year, Nova does indeed take advantage of NASPAA's failure to specify a minimum period of full-time study in its 1975 doctoral guidelines. Academicians are entirely correct in being concerned with the fact that in 1979 Nova granted 59 percent of all DPA degrees (62 to 105) and 31 percent of all doctorates (DPA and Ph.D combined, 62 of 199) in public administration.

Does this mean that the other 43 DPA degrees awarded in 1979, some of them by nontraditional programs, should be suspect by association? Does it even mean that all Nova degrees are counterfeit?

Nontraditional programs do provide a greater opportunity for cheating in the academic process. When the state boards of education in Georgia, Michigan, and North Carolina denied applications by Nova to offer its graduate program in public administration in those states, all cited examples of relaxed academic standards. Georgia state board of education spokesman Jerry D. Roseberry, for example, said Nova "lacked a strict, discriminating admissions policy." He said student work "indicated a superficial review of theory and practice in cases," and that "instructors aren't directly involved and can't provide the necessary guidance, assistance, and direction" during the final stages of the program.[1] Yet the vote against granting the license was 5 to 4, partly because some board of education members felt Roseberry's statements are true of *most* doctoral programs in public administration, both traditional and nontraditional.

Whatever the merits of Nova's programs, it is unfair to tar all nontraditional programs with the Nova brush. Neither is it appropriate to denigrate the DPA degree as a mere practitioner's degree as long as scholars such as Frederick C. Mosher (DPA, Harvard, 1953) are receiving the Dwight Waldo Award of the American Society for Public Administration for "distinguished contributions to the literature of public administration."

It is difficult to discern the motives of a Nova, a Walden, an Oklahoma, a Maryland, a Southern California, or a Virginia Tech. Are they in off-campus education just for the money? In the first two cases, the answer is probably yes. In the next two, it is probably yes and no. In the last two, it is probably no. The entrepreneurs at Nova and Walden discovered how to make nontraditional education pay. Those at Oklahoma and Maryland saw that advantage, too, but they also saw a legitimate educational mission—to take education to people in comparatively isolated places, particularly military bases. Public administrationists at Southern California and Virginia Tech are genuine exponents of the new public administration, of the importance of equity and advocacy in modern public administration. They feel an obligation to gain a maximum amount of informed citizen participation in the decision-making processes of government and to make educational services available to all as activities in the public interest and for the public good. Such distinctions as these are important.

The continuum extends even further, however, to such institutions as the University of Colorado and Western Michigan University. They represent yet another type of nontraditional graduate program in public administration. Each school makes a DPA program available at the state capital, some distance from the main campus. Each school also makes an MPA program available at locations two driving hours or less from the main campus, but still within the state. The programs are demonstrably rigorous and academically successful, yet they do not meet two of the traditional criteria of quality programs. Faculty are not in residence at Western's regional training centers, for example. Adjunct faculty are occasionally used. The great majority of the students are part time. Main campus faculty members travel to the regional training centers at least twice a week, however. There are frequent telephone calls, and there is close coordination. The students are adult learners. They are frequently public servants who are as informed as the professor in given areas. They demand that the professor be prepared for class. And they often say in course evaluations: "This course was a lot tougher, more interesting, and more relevant than the one I got on campus 12 years ago. Thanks."

In attempting to draw the distinction between those who may abuse the idea and the forms of nontraditional education and those who try to use them as instruments of public service, one is reminded of Woodrow Wilson's discussion of the opportunity to learn administration from the Prussian and French autocracies of the 1880s. "If I see a murderous fellow sharpening a knife cleverly," he wrote, "I can borrow his way of sharpening the knife without borrowing his probable intention to commit murder with it; and so, if I see a monarchist dyed in the wool managing a public bureau well, I can learn his business methods without changing one of my republican spots." [2]

A paraphrase of the Wilson quotation might be: "If I see a greedy fellow cleverly manipulating a new idea about how to do education, I can borrow his way of delivering his product without borrowing his probable intention of making money at the expense of academic standards; and so, if I see a Nova University administrator dyed in the wool managing an off-campus program well, I can learn his business methods without changing one of my NASPAA spots."

Education beyond Training

The third distinction suggesting itself is based on the discussion in Chapter 1 of the professional socialization role of the professor. I am not in basic disagreement with the author's position, but I wish to vary the spectrum.

Personal contact between professor and student is indeed the sine qua non of qualitative learning. Computer-based technology will eventually remove most of the logistical barriers of access to information, but how much more is learning than information gathering! Particularly in public administration, the quantitative tools we put in the manager's tool kit are not enough to deal with the conundrums which occupy much of the manager's time and place heavy demands on his discretion. Knowledge *and* power are the stuff of public administration.

What are the characteristics of professional behavior in this context? It is true that many nontraditional programs duck the problem. "We're here to train you in management information systems, budgetary analysis techniques, and personnel management processes. If you want ethics, go to a philosophy department." This may be training, but education goes well beyond training.

Insofar as nontraditional education programs merely train, and avoid professional education, they are remiss in their total responsibility to students. Yet there is no data to support the idea that traditional campus-based programs are any better at exercising this responsibility than nontraditional programs. Indeed, the most recent data suggest that nobody does it. After surveying 219 schools and programs in public policy and public administration, Joel L. Fleishman and Bruce L. Payne reported in 1980 that "Nowhere, however, do courses in which ethical issues are central make up as much as 10 percent of the curriculum, and it is probably fair to say that a substantial majority of policy students graduate with no formal training in the subject."[3]

If professional standards and ethics are not built into the curriculum of either the traditional or nontraditional program in public administration, the bearer of the ark of professional covenants must therefore be the individual instructor. Whatever value system he or she represents will be communicated to students. It will sometimes be embraced, and sometimes contested, by them.

This distinction is more subtle than the obvious fact that traditional institutions are no better equipped to provide role models than nontraditional ones. It has to do with the fact that professors, particularly elitist professors, are often less knowledgeable about the requirements of professionalism than the mature student in the nontraditional classroom. In an environment of participatory democracy, the educable professor will learn that professional socialization has already taken place among these students and that his or her most productive role may be that of facilitator and practical idealist. The professor may choose to retreat to the original meaning of the teaching role. He may merely profess, or confess, the truth as he has come to know it. In any case, the professor's manner is crucial.

If the above is true, it follows that the verbal and nonverbal transactions between teacher and student which are fundamental to the transplanting of ideas and attitudes can take place anywhere—in Fayerweather Hall at Columbia, in the Woodrow Wilson School at Princeton, or in the basement of the Bureau of Management and Staff Development Building in Lansing. In the professional socialization role of the professor, environment is more important than place. Everyone in the classroom learns from everyone else. Education is not just the dispensing of information. It is the discovery of the self.

Public Administration as a Marketplace Phenomenon

The author of this reflective piece is worried that the profession's reputation is suffering because of ambiguities in NASPAA's standards and guidelines for doctoral programs. He is concerned about substandard or completely standardized mass production processes in public administration education, and that "we may be preparing persons to deliver public services in a similar slipshod manner with no thought given to individual needs and differences." It is a service to the profession that people worry about such things.

I would caution that such concerns can become self-fulfilling prophecies if not tempered by recognition of the unique characteristics of public administration itself. We are a marketplace phenomenon. The best line of the article is that we do unto others. But we do unto others where they are. We are on the front lines of change and innovation, and we shoot at the moving target of the public interest. We are eclectic, and we are a holding company of disparate professional groups and academic disciplines. Because we live up front, we must not judge ourselves more harshly than we deserve.

Contra Elitism

The hierarchical baggage of the medieval university is no longer appropriate for a large slice of American education. Nontraditional education gives people of all ages and conditions of life the chance to taste the great works and the great ideas of Western civilization. Students in nontraditional classrooms are there with high expectations, maturity, and discipline. They have a keen desire to share professional skills and knowledge. They cannot be expected to fit into the traditional pattern of college as a kind of extended adolescence, with neither the rights nor the responsibilities of adulthood. They change the social dynamics of the classroom. They are experienced consumers, eager to play a role in shaping their education and ready to switch schools, programs, or courses if their needs are not met. They make certain of what is expected of them. They are concerned about grades and are not reticent about questioning them. In turn, they evaluate their instructors seriously and thoughtfully.

It is appropriate that public administration programming and instruction has taken a place in this movement of equity. Let us learn from recent history and not go the way of the American Political Science Association, whose steadily diminishing numbers by 1981 make it only about half the size of the American Society for Public Administration. The reasons for the APSA decline are not hard to find: elitism, exclusiveness, preoccupation with academic purity and old boy networking, and a refusal to listen to voices of advocacy on the left. The day public administration reaches such establishmentarianism will be the day its own decline begins. Let us postpone that day as long as possible.

Notes

1. Roseberry, J. D. in "Georgia Rejects Nova Bid to Offer DPA Programs. *Public Administration Times,* May 1, 1980, p. 8.
2. Wilson, W. "The Study of Administration." *Political Science Quarterly 2* (June, 1887):219–220.
3. Fleishman, J. L. and Payne, B. L. *Ethical Dilemmas and the Education of Policymakers,* (Hastings-on-Hudson, New York, The Hastings Center, 1980), p. 3.

3
Rejoinder to Chandler

William Earle Klay
Florida State University, Tallahassee, Florida

It is not easy to write a rejoinder to comments with which one largely agrees. I am especially thankful for Professor Chandler's thoughtful observations regarding socialization but it is, nevertheless, important that I clarify some misimpressions about other points. His thrust seems to imply that I am opposed to the nontraditional. Having just proposed that public administration become a pioneer in placing much of its literature into universally accessible computer storage, I find this implication puzzling. Public administration is faced with a challenging obligation to provide education to thousands of nontraditional students. This obligation can be met only through careful, measured innovation.

Quality may be absent from some traditional programs and present in some nontraditional ones. My intention is not to deny this nor to deny the great variation which now exists among nontraditional programs, but to propose a framework for more fully evaluating all of our educational programs. Much must be done to better evaluate the outcomes of traditional programs, but we are doing ourselves a disservice as a profession if we think that we are unable to recognize quality when it exists. A quality program is one which effectively imparts skills and conveys much knowledge from our literature, and which does so through a faculty who also convey a devotion to high standards of performance, a genuine concern for the needs of each individual, and a willingness to bear the "ark of professional convenants."

I submit that we know less about what is necessary to attain quality in nontraditional programs, and for this reason it is the innovators who are most obligated to evaluate what they are doing. It is unfortunate that this evaluation must be done in an atmosphere of growing crisis regarding the credibility of one of our degrees—the DPA. It is certainly not my intention to denigrate the DPA, for I am a proud holder of that degree from the University of Georgia. It must be recognized, however, that NASPAA's failure to come to grips with the problem of standards in doctoral education is contributing to the DPA crisis, a crisis for which Nova University is largely to blame.

There are, and should be, numerous differences between doctorates in political science and those in public administration. It is not at all clear, however, as to what the differences, if any, should be between the two doctorates in public administration. I have reviewed the published requirements for most of these programs and find that the differences are often minor or indistinguishable. The fields and courses required are essentially the same in most instances and a Ph.D. can be obtained at some institutions on a part-time basis with no language required. The recipient of a Ph.D. in our profession should certainly learn about advanced management techniques and be knowledgeable about the subleties of implementation. Conversely, for a DPA recipient not to be qualified to do very sophisticated research in organizations is to deny the thrust toward the fuller use of research which is evident in our literature and which is already reflected in the better MPA programs.

Do our obligations to provide education for administrators include offering a doctorate under conditions which depart sharply from a full-time effort? I personally have my doubts and suspect that we should, instead, be doing more to press public agencies and prospective students to take extended leaves of absence. What concerns me most, however, is that the ambiguity of NASPAA standards regarding the DPA, and the profession's continuing reluctance to evaluate its own programs has already caused irreparable harm to a respected degree.

If the DPA degree is, as NASPAA guidelines indicate, supposed to be as rigorous as the Ph.D., then perhaps we should do as Syracuse University did and retroactively convert most DPA's to Ph.D.'s. A post-master's certificate such as the specialist in education degree could be instituted for persons who cannot spend the full-time effort which the existing guidelines say both degrees require . . . or is it necessary to offer the credential of "doctor" to induce administrators to do post-master's study? I hope not. We must be innovative but we must also take care lest we be guilty of bowing to credentialism or of preaching what we do not practice insofar as program evaluation is concerned.

4

Lost in the Management Jungle: women and administrative theory

Naomi B. Lynn
Kansas State University, Manhattan, Kansas

One of the challenges confronting public administration education in the 1980s is the preparation of students for the emergence of women in administration. The indications are that women are slowly but inevitably taking their place within that previously all-male enclave known as management. Are we as educators preparing our students for these changes? We have been challenged by Frederick Mosher to remember that "it is doubtful there is any element in any evolving culture more significant for the nature of the public service than the educational system, both formal and informal, by which are transmitted its ethos, frames of reference, and knowledge, and partly through which they are changed and knowledge enlarged."[1] Are we confronting the issues raised by the entry of women into public management in our lectures, assigned readings, and theoretical discussions? Education that does not meet this challenge serves to perpetuate the status quo and to reinforce the structural characteristics that have contributed to women's subordinate role in organizations. We do not know the effect of stereotypical attitudes on actual behavior, but we can assume that they have some impact and that an awareness of the problem should have some positive results. Education that does not meet this challenge fails to prepare students adequately for the changing roles confronting both sexes. Education that does not meet this challenge acknowledges an unwillingness to reflect societal change, and inevitably will become outdated and intellectually stagnant. This chapter will present a short version of a larger forthcoming study that examines public administration education and reflects on how the subject of women can and should be incorporated into the administrative curriculum.

Textbooks

Much of what is learned in courses is determined by the textbook selected by the professor. Ellen Cannon and Valerie Sims surveyed seven of the most frequently assigned public administration textbooks. They were interested in whether or how these texts treated women.[2] They found that little attention was paid to women and that such emphasis as occurred was primarily in the public personnel section. Lest one assume that public personnel textbooks compensate for the failures of the public administration textbooks, it should be observed that one of the best-known personnel books, Stahl's *Public Personnel Administration*, barely acknowledges the existence of women, and two of its references to women are followed by warnings against "misguided efforts to acquire quick 'representativeness' in public sector agencies" and statements of concern that the "zeal to ensure fairness and opportunity to all must not be prostituted so that lesser competence is elevated over greater competence."[3]

When women were discussed in the textbooks surveyed by Cannon and Sims, it was in the context of affirmative action with little distinction made between women and minorities. The textbook authors did not manifest any sensitivity to the institutional differences between sexism and racism. The dearth of attention and understanding about women's issues found in the textbooks illustrates the failure of public administration education to prepare students of both sexes for dealing effectively and thoughtfully with this major issue of the 1980s. If similar principles apply to men and women in an administrative context, the lack of distinction need pose no problem. For the present and foreseeable future, however, there are and will be important differences between the sexes as managers. We will consider the nature and significance of these differences as they apply both to educators and practitioners.

The Management Theory Jungle Reexamined

In 1961 Harold Koontz wrote a much heralded article that attempted to make some order out of the diverse theories of management prevalent at that time.[4] He titled his article "The Management Theory Jungle." There is another kind of jungle that exists today, but it is a barren jungle characterized by little academic growth. The various management approaches that have resulted from the developments in administrative theory have paid little or no attention to the implications of these approaches for explaining the status of women in organizations. One reason administrative theory is taught is to help students understand why people behave the way they do in organizations. If this is a major goal, it is difficult to justify the neglect women have received from administrative theorists. There is much virgin territory for research in this area, but the lack of a body of findings thus far does not excuse the classroom teacher from becoming familiar with the contributions from sociology, psychology, and economics that have implications for administrative theory. It should not prevent the professor from reexamining prevailing theories to discover biases or potential reinterpretations, or even simply using these theories as springboards for discussion to stimulate analysis, judgement, and evaluation.

Behavioral Management Approach

Most courses in administrative theory acknowledge the contributions made by Chris Argyris.[5] Argyris has written extensively about what the organization does to human developmental trends. He observes that human beings tend to develop from a state of passivity as infants to a state of increasing activity as adults; from a state of dependence to relative independence; from being capable of behaving only in a few ways to being capable of behaving in many different ways. Human beings, according to Argyris, develop from having erratic, casual, shallow, quickly changed interests to deeper interests, from short- to long-term perspective; from being in a subordinate position in the family and society to being equal or superordinate. They gradually displace their lack of awareness of self with control over self as an adult. How often have these processes been discussed in class without the observation that these trends of human development have a different impact on males and females. Societal expectations about the proper location for a healthy individual along the immature-mature continuum are quite different for males and females. One significant study found that clinicians tend to ascribe different attributes when describing healthy males and females.[6] (It is worth noting that the traits for "healthy" women are negatively associated with most positive characteristics of managers—more submissive, less independent, more easily influenced, less aggressive, less competitive, more excitable in a minor crisis, more emotional, and less objective.)

If, as Argyris argues, the organization has a tendency to treat workers as if they were children, this will probably be much more true for women, since such treatment is more compatible with cultural expectations and norms. Some women may find this acceptable because they have internalized the values this treatment represents. The result for other women may be a more intensified experience of frustration, conflict, failure, and short time perspective than that experienced by male colleagues. Argyris points out that the degree of passivity, dependence, and submissiveness tends to increase as one goes down the line of command.[7] And of course as one goes down the line of command, one is more likely to encounter women. Failure to treat individuals as healthy adults, Argyris points out, may cause the employee to (1) lose interest in his or her work, (2) lose self-confidence, (3) give up quickly, (4) lower work standards, (5) fear new tasks, (6) expect more failure, and (7) develop a tendency to blame others.[8] The reader will have no difficulty identifying Argyris's observations with stereotypically alleged descriptions of many female employees. Students should be asked to discuss how much behavior attributed to female workers is a function of their more common location in the lower reaches of the organizational system. To discuss Argyris without taking advantage of the opportunity to relate the concepts to female work behavior is to abdicate the responsibility to prepare effective managers for the 1980s.

Theory X and Theory Y Revisited

Another theorist who receives considerable attention in public administration is Douglas McGregor. McGregor observes that behind every managerial decision or action are assumptions about human nature and human behavior. He labels his two basic management theories Theory X and Theory Y.[9] Today we should be acknowledging that among managers there are also some basic assumptions about the nature of women that influence management policies and practices. The first and traditional view we will call Theory F. Theory F is based on the following assumptions:

1. Woman's proper and primary function is to be wife and mother.
2. Women are biologically and psychologically unsuited for leadership, i.e., management roles.
3. Women's jobs are usually simple, require little skill, and are unsuitable for men.
4. Even if one found an "exceptional" woman, men would not accept her as a manager. Probably the woman's subordinates would not accept her either.

Like Theory X, Theory F has deep roots. One need only examine the writings of fundamentalist theologians to discover the biblical rationale that underpins the belief in the traditional role for women. Numerous other cultural, economic, and social institutions provide further support for these premises. Like Theory X, Theory F materially influences managerial strategy in a large number of organizations. Like Theory X, Theory F prevents our seeing the other possibilities inherent in other management strategies. Like Theory X, the assumptions of Theory F prevent us from discovering, let alone utilizing, the potentialities of the average able woman.

In recent years we have started to question old assumptions about women and management. These old assumptions are being replaced by new ones that we can label Theory A. Theory A is based on the following assumptions:

1. Individuals should be permitted to make career choices not restricted by traditional or stereotypic expectations.
2. Managerial potential is distributed equally between the two sexes.
3. What is described as "female work behavior" is a response to situational factors and is not necessarily sex related.
4. The problems associated with women managers are largely the results of their small number, and can be solved by expanding the opportunities available for women.
5. Both organizations and all of society benefit when individuals are judged on merit and not on the accident of birth.

Theory A, like Theory Y, indicates the possibility of human growth and development. Under Theory F, when women do not advance, it is easy to rationalize that it is they who are at fault for attempting to compete and operate in a sphere alien to their natural roles. Women are expected to fail and the cycle of the self-fulfilling prophecy comes into play. Under Theory A, if women do not advance the manager is forced to reexamine the organization and identify the structures that are inhibiting progress. Theory F makes acceptance of the status quo comfortable; Theory A invites challenge and innovation.

Individual Behavior and Group Socialization

The behavioral management approach, as well as its predecessor the human
relations school, has divided itself into the interpersonal behavior approach
with the emphasis on individual psychology and the group behavior approach
with the emphasis on group behavior patterns.[10] Most public administration
courses with an emphasis on organizational behavior discuss both approaches.
Students need to be aware of the implications for women inherent in these
two sets of assumptions.

The premises of individual psychology support the contention that women,
as a result of socialization or predisposition, develop traits and behavior patterns that limit their effectiveness as managers. If this theory is accepted,
then women need to be resocialized if they are going to compete successfully
for top level positions. The dilemma is that sex differences based on socialization findings may not have been controlled for intervening variables used
to explain the results. For example, studies have shown that sex differences
disappear when experience, type of organization, level, and professional training are controlled.[11] The "socialization as cause" findings may thus be the
results of what Caplan and Nelson have termed the "person-blame causal
attribution bias in psychological research"; that is, "research that focuses on
person-centered characteristics while ignoring situationally relevant factors."[12]
The issue is not merely of academic interest because as Caplan and Nelson
observe, "The way a problem is defined determines not only what is done
about it, but also what is not done—or apparently need not be done."[13] In
terms of our discussion, if one blames early socialization, one also accepts the
futility of doing anything about the situation.

The group behavior approach receives much of its insight from sociology
and anthropology. Unlike the person-blame perspective, sociologists do not
believe that it is always necessary to change the person to solve the problem.
The sociological assumption is that people's attitudes are shaped at least as
much by the organization in which they work as by their preexisting
attitudes.[14] Kanter, a sociologist, explains female work behavior and experience partially on the basis of the social composition of groups.[15] She observes that women in management tend to be in "skewed" groups, that is,
they are heavily outnumbered so they are not treated as individuals, but as
representatives of their groups—tokens. As tokens they are scrutinized and
talked about much more than their male colleagues. The reminder that they
are "different" often keeps women from performing at their best. Pressure
is put on the woman not to "show up" the dominant. They have to find that
fine line between doing well but not too well. This is the price they have to

pay for the peer acceptance necessary for success. Their behavior is not unlike that of minorities, who also have to play out the stereotype role to gain
acceptance.[16] This structural perspective does not emphasize the nature of
personalities in organizations, but rather the structures in which roles are
performed. It examines the environment and climate of organizations and
how the norms and expectations determine the nature of the organization,
and how behavior is affected by factors such as the existing opportunity
structure.

The Managerial Role Approach

Henry Mintzberg has taken issue with the management process school that
describes the functions of managers as planning, organizing, coordinating, and
controlling.[17] Mintzberg says that what managers really do is act out a set of
ten roles, and how effectively they carry out these roles determines their
managerial success or failure.

The ten roles are:

Interpersonal Roles – Figurehead, Leader, Liaison
Informational Roles – Monitor, Disseminator, Spokesman
Decisional Roles – Entrepreneur, Disturbance Handler, Resource Allocator,
    Negotiator.

These ten roles, Mintzberg says, suggest a number of important management skills such as developing peer relationships, carrying out negotiations,
motivating subordinates, resolving conflicts, establishing information net-
works, and allocating resources. These skills, Mintzberg says, can be practiced
through techniques such as role playing. He suggests further that management schools can enhance managerial skills by encouraging sensible risk taking
and innovation. This is undoubtedly good advice, but the caveat should be
raised that this will be effective only if the professor is sensitive to the special
implications this may have for women.

Let us examine just three of the roles described by Mintzberg where
women may find they are at a disadvantage: *monitor, resources allocator,*
and *negotiator*. As monitor, the manager constantly searches the environment for information, questions his or her peers and subordinates, and receives much unsolicited information as a result of personal contacts.[18] It has
been observed that women are less likely to be part of the informal network
that provides much of the information that would make them effective mon-
itors. Kanter also observes that women are often not viewed as being informed

beyond the technical requirements of the job. This may be true and a consequence of women in high management positions coming in from the outside rather than through the ranks.[19] The newly established Senior Executive Service makes it easier for individuals to enter the federal bureaucracy at the top. One of the justifications for this was to permit more women to enter top level federal positions. These women may find themselves at a disadvantage as they attempt to use the monitor role to generate power.

As a resource allocator, the manager determines who will get what in his or her agency. The more resources the manager controls, and can hence distribute, the more effective he or she will be. Often women are not given the control over resources to which their formal positions entitle them because their superiors lack confidence in them, and the overprotecting of female managerial employees may work to undermine their authority and power, by letting subordinates know that they have no resources under their control to distribute.

An important management role is that of *negotiator*. The negotiator represents the organization in working out compromises and differences between the organization and other agencies, unions, and subordinates. How effective can a negotiator be who is not at the nerve center of the needed information and whose authority to commit organizational resources has been undermined by her superior? The undermining may be done by overprotecting women or allowing her to be bypassed by her subordinate, or by overreacting to every negative comment made about her.[20] This kind of environment is hardly conducive to the taking of risks encouraged by Mintzberg.

Contingency Approach

The contingency approach is based on the assumption that there is no single solution that is best for all situations. What is done in actual practice depends on a given set of circumstances. Some situations call for action that in a different setting would not be productive. Contingency theory therefore assumes that there are no principles of management that are universal, but rather factors that have to be examined in determining management strategies, such as the environment, the organizational structure, and human resources. Three of the roles discussed above, that of monitor, resource allocator, and negotiator are to a large extent determined by how effective one is at playing the more critical leadership role. Leadership theory should not be discussed without acknowledging specific issues resulting from lack of opportunity to succeed, actual versus formal power, and the problem of tokenism. When leadership is not discussed in this type of contingency framework, a woman may blame herself because she has not succeeded after attempting to practice what she learned about effective leadership. Part of her theoretical training should include the knowledge that contingencies and not her personal traits may be causing the problem. Only when she and her superiors have this insight can a solution be sought. For as Mintzberg observes, "The manager's effectiveness is significantly influenced by his insight into his own work" and "Managers who can be introspective about their work are likely to be effective at their jobs." [21]

Educational Implications

I have only mentioned a few of the approaches used to teach public management. Teachers are encouraged to examine their textbooks and notes to find opportunities to relate these and other theories to the realities of female participation in the workplace. Some may argue that education will not have much impact on what actually takes place in organizations. But even those who are convinced of the impotence of education in effecting change should be aware of ongoing research in the area of sex-related organizational behavior and should assume a responsibility for encouraging students to become sensitive to one of the most significant revolutions of our time—the changing female role.

Notes

1. Mosher, C. *Democracy and Public Service*. Oxford University Press, New York, 1968, p. 25.
2. Cannon, E. and Sims, V. Public Administration: Alice in Wonderland. *News For Teachers of Political Science 27* (Fall, 1980):2-4.
3. Stahl, G. *Public Personnel Administration*. Harper and Row, New York, 1976, p. 167.
4. Koontz, H. The Management Theory Jungle. *Academy of Management Journal 4* (1961):174-188.
5. Argyris, C. *Personality and Organization*. Harper and Brothers, New York, 1957.
6. Broverman, I. K., Broverman, D. M., Clarkson, F. E., Rosenkrantz, P. S., Vogel, S. R. Sex Role Stereotypes and Clinical Judgments of Mental Health. *Journal of Consulting and Clinical Psychology 34* (February, 1970):1-7.

7. Argyris, p. 77.
8. Argyris, p. 78.
9. McGregor, E. *The Human Side of Enterprise.* McGraw-Hill, New York, 1960.
10. Koontz, H. The Management Theory Jungle Revisited. *Academy of Management Review 5* (April, 1978):175–187.
11. Osborn, R. N., Vicars, W. M. Sex Stereotypes: An Artifact in Leader Behavior and Subordinate Satisfaction Analysis? *Academy of Management Journal 19* (September, 1976):439–449; Bartol, K. M. Sex Effects in Evaluating Leaders. *Journal of Applied Psychology 61* August, 1976):446–454; Brief, A. P., Oliver, R. L. Male-Female Differences in Work Attitudes among Retail Sales Managers. *Journal of Applied Psychology 61* (August, 1976):526–528; Renwich, P. A. The Effects of Sex Differences on the Perception and Management of Superior-Subordinate Conflict: An Exploratory Study. *Organizational Behavior and Human Performance 21* (1978):403–415.
12. Caplan, N. and Nelson, S. D. On Being Useful: The Nature and Consequences of Psychological Research on Social Problems. *American Psychologist 28* (March, 1973):199.
13. Caplan and Nelson, p. 201.
14. Perrow, C. B. *Organizational Analysis: A Sociological View.* Brooks/Cole Publishing Company, Belmont, Calif., 1970, p. 4.
15. Kanter, R. M. *Men and Women of the Corporation.* Basic Books, New York, 1977, pp. 208, 209.
16. Kanter, p. 211.
17. Mintzberg, H. The Manager's Job: Folklore and Fact. *Harvard Business Review 53* (1975):49–61.
18. Mintzberg, p. 56.
19. Kanter, R. M. Power Failure in Management Circuits. *Harvard Business Review 57* (July, 1979):65–68.
20. Kanter, Power Failure in Management Circuits, p. 69.
21. Mintzberg, p. 60.

5
Institutional Problems of Public Administration Programs: a house without a home

James S. Bowman
Florida State University, Tallahassee, Florida

Jeremy F. Plant
George Mason University, Fairfax, Virginia

Taxpayer revolts and a conservative administration in Washington notwith-standing, American government has attained unprecedented size and influence. Its scope and magnitude, and the knowledge and skills needed for effective management have increased the quantity and quality of educational programs in public affairs and public administration. Yet due to the Jacksonian philosophy of the citizen administrator, the diverse nature of government employment, and, more recently, questions about the contribution of schools of administration to the profession, education for the public service has never been widely accepted in the United States.[1]

Nonetheless, during the 1970s both the practice and teaching of public administration experienced a kind of coming of age.[2] The last decade witnessed a rush by most of the nation's universities to become identified in some way with the field. In a time of retrenchment, the emergence and growth of programs in public management have been a significant development in higher education. Harvard University President Derek C. Bok summarized that nature of the challenge by declaring that nothing less than the education of an entire profession was needed.[3]

As the number of programs has grown, so has the diversity of organizational arrangements; colleges and universities are characterized by a variety of schools, institutes, centers, divisions, and departments of public administration/affairs/policy. Indeed, one of the reasons that the National Association of Schools of Public Affairs and Administration (NASPAA) was created was to deal with problems caused by this variation.

The lack of a general consensus about the structure of education for the public service is demonstrated by the fact that professional competencies for administration are not well defined. There is no core of knowledge, no firm boundaries for the discipline, or even a definition of what it is.[4,5] In short, for all the growth in the field, there are few programs that have the strength and coherence comparable to those serving other professions.

These issues seem real to most public administrationists because, it almost goes without saying, they believe that structural as well as substantive issues are worth attention. In an area of study where one may choose from 2 to 11 or more areas of concentration and where there is little or no consistency in course requirements from school to school,[6] some order in the apparent chaos may nonetheless be found. Several structural considerations seem evident.

First, despite diversity, three program models—public administration, public management, and public policy—comprehend most educational programs in the field.[7] There are significant variations within each, but they are variations on a theme.[8-11] Second, the intellectual basis of public administration, such as it is, has remained remarkably constant over the years. As many observers have noted,[12-14] public administration and its subfields of personnel administration, budgeting, and organization and management have proven to be quite resilient. A fourth subfield, policy analysis and evaluation, is now an integral part of any well-designed program.

Unlike some commentators, the present authors do not believe that the future of education for the public service is in serious doubt[15] nor that the time for public administration is past.[16] As long as the state survives, bureaucracy is not likely to fade into insignificance. But mere existence is not the same as the mature development of the field. As Louis C. Gawthrop has noted,[17] the real question was raised by Woodrow Wilson nearly 100 years ago: "How can we best prepare individuals for the public service?" In an effort to address this question, this analysis will (1) briefly trace the evolution of public administration education, (2) examine in some detail the problematic structure of public administration programs, and explore solutions to those problems, and (3) conclude with observations that transcend structural issues.

Evolution of Public Administration Education

One of the principal conclusions from a recent history of the discipline was
that its evolution and growth has been dependent upon and responsive to the
social and intellectual environment. Indeed, it has been argued that public
administration was, for the most part, an American invention.[18]

As a pioneer of American public administration, Woodrow Wilson was
concerned with the nation's effort to reconcile democracy with administration. One of the first to recognize that modern government was largely
administration—that discretion meant the authoritative allocation of values—
he noted in an oft-quoted phrase that it was "getting harder to *run* a con-
stitution than to frame one."[19,20] To run a democratic state, politics must
control administration, but popular will and efficient administration could be
subverted if politics became too partisan. Public administration could be seen
as an instrument of the chief executive to achieve and assure a higher form of
civilization. Like the founders of other social sciences, early political scientists often aspired to a new science of morality. Ill-served by the spoilsman
and an ad hoc approach to public management, partisan political administration had to be transformed into professional public administration.

Public administration, therefore, should not only be separate from politics,
but scientific as well. Modern science, under the auspices of the merit system,
could apply technical principles to the business of government. By adapting
European administration techniques to American society, democratic politics
would profit from an administratively efficient, morally irreproachable, and
politically neutral public service. Borrowing administrative procedures from
abroad would be acceptable, however, only under the constraints of political
responsibility and the scientific method.

Thus, although the political and the administrative can be separated for
purposes of scientific analysis and political reform, they are inseparable in
operation. Wilson was not ignoring reality in government, but distinguishing
its essential components. His concept of the study of administration was that
it was an integral part of government and the greater realm of philosophy and
ethics. Nevertheless, due to the ambiguities and contradictions in Wilson's
classic article, and later oversimplifications of it, a politics-administration
dualism was born in the name of good government.

With the spoils system still in flower, civil service reformers and administrative theorists insisted that administration could be divorced from politics.
Encouraged by the scientific management movement, nearly all professional
students of public administration adopted the view that a value-free science
of administration could be developed. The politics-administration distinction,

which was devolving into a rigid dichotomy, provided a theory of administration in democracy. As such, it could and did replace the spoils system as political orthodoxy.

In a time of great concern over professional status and confidence in the scientific method, the abdication of social responsibility that accompanied the abandonment of values became one of the casualties of the period. Political science made the fateful shift toward a science and disciplinary model and away from the professional model. Undergirded by the dichotomy concept, the study of government evolved with little attention to political ethics or social purpose. Value-free inquiry promised to discover verifiable laws of politics. Scholars interested in the organization of government, eschewing overt reformist ambitions, drew their inspiration from business management and ultimately developed scientific principles of administration. Laws of political behavior and principles of administration would form the modern science of government. The era increasingly looked like the Iron Cage prophesized by Max Weber, as little critical attention was paid to the growing Leviathan that provided social prestige and financial support to the profession.

The demise of the politics-administration dichotomy in the 1940s, the suspicion of value-free science during the 1960s, and the contemporary crisis of confidence in American society have converged to make it evident that the theoretician and practitioner of public administration form decisions on the basis of both science and morality. Nicholas Henry has stated that this recognition produced "a disquieting notion that a sense of ethics was a genuine need in the profession."[21] Disquieting because there has been no "clarion call"[22] capable of directing public service education toward a set of agreed-upon goals. The unity of consciousness that energized the profession in its early years has long since dissipated. The field has been left with no unifying end and is guided by no integrated theory.

Educationally, the result of this state of affairs is that an instrumental approach to public administration has been emphasized.[23] If the 1967 Honey Report on Higher Education for Public Service sparked the feeling that public administration had little to say about contemporary issues and problems,[24] the National Academy of Public Administration's Watergate Report[25] provided even less direction in an era of crisis. The field seemed very much interested in educating students to "do" public service, but not necessarily to "be" public servants.[26] In a word, although public administration continued to grow, its intellectual and structural development has been in disarray due to the destruction of its doctrinal foundations.

The perspective demanded by public administration's environment today extends well beyond the mechanistic, classical approach. Despite the key role universities play in developing the public service, academic preparation generally demonstrates little recognition of it.[27] Most future civil servants are trained as specialists with only perfunctory attention to the public setting where their expertise will be applied. Clearly there is a greater need to understand the status and role of the professions in public life. The challenge for universities is to introduce and nurture such a consciousness at an early stage of professional training. Yet there have been few studies of this problem. There is, for example, little information regarding what administrators think about their professional education and how it could be improved.[28,29]

The central problem of self-conscious public administration has always been in defining a sense of purpose that could be comfortably accommodated within the basic tenets of democratic theory.[30] A new sense of meaning must evolve if public administration is to become certain of its role in American government. A public administration characterized by an awareness of a purposeful future is a practical necessity given the public policy complexities confronting government.

The increasing breadth and depth of knowledge in public administration, the high degree of policy analysis and evaluation required, and the explicit function of ethics in the civil service may suggest a new sense of purpose. As Brewster C. Denny has pointed out, schools of administration are special and distinctive; they may not be the only place in institutions of higher learning where public policy and administration are studied, but they are the only place that does only that.[31]

An orientation that looks to the long-term humanization and improvement of the public service inevitably involves risk, but that is certainly in the best tradition of the academy. A recent survey of MPA graduates found that the field has a deep reservoir of support from which to draw.[32] Perhaps one reason for the structural difficulties discussed below is that risks are especially dangerous in an era of retrenchment. Yet, given the support for NASPAA guidelines,[33] the field may be closer to answers about questions in the education of the profession than is generally recognized. Since it is probably not possible to resolve all intellectual issues first, what structures are now in use which may—or may not—encourage their resolution?

The Problematic Structure of Public Administration Education

The writings of Dwight Waldo are a good place to start, since much of his concern is with the institutional home of public administration. Using

NASPAA institutions as the data base,[34,35] he finds that approximately two-fifths of all programs are housed in political science departments and the rest scattered among schools of public administration/affairs, business, generic management, and public policy. Robert Golembiewski develops a comparable list based on the same orienting factor: that institutional housing of programs will vary, and with it a presumption of different outcomes.[36] That this variety seems to be a relatively fixed universe is further shown by a recent survey of undergraduate programs.[37]

The important question about this is: "Do the categories have real predictive value in understanding what is likely to happen in the educational process they engender?" That is, do they have a clear-cut idea of goals and the means to reach them, or, are they simply examples of nominalism and creeping "hardening of the categories?" Are the programs in fact *programs* with fixed goals, a path of implementation along which quantified milestones can be charted and some idea of expected outcomes? Or, will their reification lead to what some critics have called our "intense and perplexing curriculum discussions" due to a confusion of goals? [38]

Research into the internal structure of one of the categories, generic schools of management, has revealed the diversity of course offerings.[39] One might expect, therefore, that systematic examination of the others may well have a similar result.[40] Even pluralists in the field must wonder about the utility, predictive capacity, and professional virtue of structural variety based primarily on administrative battles within universities. Do alternative institutional homes contribute to the viability of well-thought-out models of public administration education? If not, what can they contribute to a professional development beyond individual skills and snippets of cognitive learning as the principal means to a holistic sense of reasoned action?[41]

Problems are compounded when certificate, undergraduate, and doctoral programs are considered beyond the traditional Masters in Public Administration (MPA). Can common goals be deduced that span this broad spectrum? In the undergraduate area, for example, three needs must be met: attending to in-service students who have reached junior management positions without the bachelors degree; preparing students to enter professional graduate programs; and providing initial professional competence to individuals preparing to enter government.[42] Certificate and doctoral programs contain a similar multiplicity of goals.

Several limited solutions to these problems exist, if it is agreed that the issue is excessive reliance upon categories that mean little to either the client (students) or the consumers (government employers) of public service education. One is to examine the nature of government administration in order to identify unities that the fixation with university arrangements and the intellectual legacy of public-administration-as-management-plus-political-science make us blind to. A good example of innovative thinking along these lines is Burgess's essay on urban administration. It is premised on the belief that the management of jurisdictions is replacing the administration of separate, uncoordinated programs. Basing his analysis on management tasks associated with jurisdictional administration, three major modes of management are identified: (1) policy management, with an emphasis on the strategic leadership function in general capacity building and the integration of organizational systems, (2) program management, or those activities needed to execute policy and achieve objectives related to goals, and (3) resource management, or those support functions (personnel management, purchasing, finance, public information) required of and related to the needs of policy and program managers.[43]

The usefulness of such an analytical model (admittedly one best suited for local government) is that it provides a structure and an agenda for an educational program. That is, it asks "What does government do and how does it do it?" and "What is the role of a trained generalist professional in this situation?" As Paul Van Riper has concluded, it is not necessary to worry about the interdisciplinary approach that this requires; it becomes self-evident that a generalist in a complicated field of action must be broadly educated.[44,45] No doubt such an approach has a certain logical elegance. It is equally without doubt that the implementation of such an amorphous concept would be a difficult, dynamic challenge for any institution builder.

A second possible solution is to forsake the deductive approach and utilize a matrix to arrange a multiplicity of topics, skill areas, or courses to meet specific needs. Promulgated by NASPAA in 1974,[46] the "matrix of professional competencies of graduates of public affairs/public administration programs and of public managers" illustrates a lack of concern for form and structure. Its major premise is the existence in the field of a consensus regarding the substance of professional skills and understanding. Structural arrangements are left open for individual schools to develop; there is no attempt at structural modeling nor does the listing of program specializations by NASPAA go beyond those areas in existing programs. Little concern is given to understanding a structure around which to justify a breakdown of concentrations within a masters program, or a set of analytical factors to guide professional development for the field.

Indeed, matrixing is often an alternative to structuring, and the NASPAA manifestation is no exception to this rule. It is a way to control and accept diversity, a critical necessity for a voluntary membership organization such

as NASPAA. Faced with the usual associational incentives for growth and
nonorthodoxy of form, NASPAA has banked on the matrix to mitigate the
structural impasses noted earlier. It bypasses both issues of institutional
arrangement and intellectual structure at the same time. NASPAA's current
MPA peer review, for instance, reflects the importance of matrixing of inputs
with little concern for structural plans to guide their utilization.

The so-called "NASPAA threat," looked at in this light may not exist, or
may be the opposite of the orthodoxy which some have envisioned as the
goal, and effect, of the association's oversight.[47] It is not a single view of
structure that is being fostered by NASPAA, but just the reverse: a variety
of approaches using either an institutional locus or intraprogram sub-
divisions.[48,49]

The developmental process of the field in the 1980s will be determined
largely by the impact of NASPAA's several projects designed to draw the
field closer together. At the moment, either committees or actual visitation
teams are in place examining acceptable limits of programs offering bachelors, masters, and doctors degrees. If NASPAA continues to use the matrix
form of analysis, it will likely bypass the question of requiring (or prohibiting)
certain types of institutional arrangements as well as requiring any proper relationship of core to subfields.[50] What may be lost in the process will be a
critical awareness of all the ramifications of the structure question.

The Structural Impasse: Toward a Comprehensive Solution

If there are problems with both the Burgess and NASPAA approaches to
structure, one way out of the structural impasse seems to be deceptively
simple. It is a decision to not allow professional activity to flounder on the
institutional questions. The book is still out on which institutional approach
works best, or even if they are based on commonly held perceptions of means
and ends relationships.

Yet the evidence is overwhelming that public administration is, and always
has been, two things: a concern with action-oriented processes of management along with a professional awareness of normative, political questions.
Stated as they usually are, the action processes seem to fall into four subfields of inquiry and professional skills development: organization and
management, finance, personnel, and policy analysis/evaluation.[51] The
professional or normative common ground so remarked by Appleby as the
essence of *public* administration[52,53] is deeply imbedded in the identity of

the field. It must be kept separate from the action-oriented subfields enough so that critical inquiry can continue on the role of (1) government in society, (2) administration in government, and (3) the individual in organizations, without sacrificing the utility of skills-grounded instruction.

Such an approach will not be easy for whoever takes it on as a goal, be it NASPAA or some other focal point in the profession. One obvious problem is the decline of the core vis-à-vis the subfield specialities, and the proliferation of the latter.[54] Proliferation of subfields is not surprising; just as government has expanded through specialized programs, so has public administration justified much of its expansion into new areas. The problem with this expansion is twofold: first, it demeans the traditions of public administration as opposed to policy-specific questions, and so makes management of programs seem a lesser and often troublesome appendage to the tasks of policy development and strategic decision making. Second, it may make it difficult to educate students for the centrist management concerns of a future dominated by jurisdictional management and interorganizational coordination. If so, the concern with a core of knowledge broadly relating governing processes to social dynamics and values—a function of the core—and managerial know-how constructed out of the updated versions of the four major process subfields may provide the needed insights for continued relevance.

A related issue may arise from the symmetry of the subfields to affect this vision of centripetality. Two subfields seem likely sources of continued concern. One is organization theory, the linear descendent of the old organization and management (O&M) formalism. It seem too big and diffuse as currently organized to support the notion that it is simply a subfield of public adminstration. There are two issues for the program designer that are endemic to organization theory. The first is focus: Should the emphasis be on applied insights or on the examination of theory and critical studies?[55] The second is the sheer volume of study: Organizations are probably the most-studied aspect of society, in part because the work on the subject has intrigued every social science. Whether a program chooses a scientific or applied perspective, the scope of the task is substantial.

The other troublesome subfield is policy analysis and evaluation. It is newer, and so less observing (or respectful) of the old balance of subfield to center, and subfield to subfield.[56,57] It makes global claims for its skills and insights and in some settings refuses to accept the other components of public administration as legitimate or relevant bodies of knowledge. Viewed in its setting within modern government, the line between managerial intelligence functions and routinized office management is often murky. Take Operations Research for example: Does it deal with problems of the O&M

sort or is it a process related to the redesign and rethinking of strategic policy? Other structural issues undoubtedly come to mind. Still, as discussed below, these problems need not be insurmountable.

Lest we seem too critical of NASPAA's planning matrix, an attractive alternative may be to modify the matrix approach to do two things: one, to require a program anatomy that goes beyond just meeting the input stew now prescribed for MPA programs. This would recognize the clear predominance of managerial processes and core concerns over horizontal additions or applications to this base, perhaps along the lines hinted at above. Two, it would make clear the separateness of public administration from other programs, and restrict use of the term "public administration" to those meeting agreed-upon goals of attention to both the public and administration foci of public administration. This would not always require a separate departmental home, but some minimum is needed for program integrity.

The separation of public administration, if that is the goal, may be either organizational or programmatic. If programmatic identity is enough, or a necessary first step, public administration educators must act as all good program managers everywhere: establish goals, milestones, and quantified indicators of success. These should relate not just to resource allocations but to real achievements. If NASPAA is to be the standard, it must establish, with our assistance, a goals and objectives statement of public administration for the 1980s and beyond. The goals might address such questions as these: What is the professional manager required to know to be effective and responsive? Is he or she to be primarily a generalist, or specialized in substantive expertise? What is the needed mix of public-administration-educated officials and other professionals? How will public administration, viewed critically as the aggregate of all programs allowed to use the name, contribute (in very predictable and real ways) to changes in the public service and in the society that public service serves?

Once a dynamic model is in place for gauging public administration's impact on its environments and clientele, the product should begin to be controlled. The final separation from political science, as dominant and unfaithful spouse, will then have been achieved: We will have positively affected the nature of the phenomenon of government, led to its taming (possibly even management), and shown that an academic program can be professionally oriented and still critical of its object. Reductionism must be avoided; public administration must push its focus beyond the narrow confines of typical executive branch bureaucracies. The goal should be to place everything known or imagined about administration into the professional and subprofessional categories that seem so enduring (and, perhaps, endearing).

This will be the response to Wilson's 100 year summons for a science of administration that is uniquely American.[58]

Conclusion

As this analysis shows, a great deal is taking place in public administration education. Answers to questions such as "are schools and programs properly structured?" are as complicated as they are controversial. The tentative approach outlined in this chapter is perhaps not demonstrably the single best of all possible worlds—but then neither is any other. Its value obtains to the extent that it engenders discussion about how public administration might be more productively modelled and developed.

It must be recognized at the conclusion of a study of this kind that the way programs are structured may have significant effects on their direction, but that the values held by public administrators and how they arrive at them are also important. Indeed, an undo emphasis on structural forms and arrangements may be just one more manifestation of the instrumental, as opposed to the normative, approach to field.[59] Since public administrators must formulate policy compatible with American principles and values, they ought to be able to develop patterns of ethical reasoning.[60] As T. Edwin Boling stresses,[61] public agencies are normative by definition and the public official's job is value-laden. The manager is, therefore, a decision-maker, a valuer.

While civil servants may be interested in discussing values,[62] most observers do not believe that they are adequately prepared to deal with such issues.[63] Not only is there little evidence to suggest that public executives hold sentiments about public life different from the rest of the American workforce, but also there are few public administration programs that sufficiently socialize their students to a career role.[64,65]

Paula Gordon has identified three types of public service behavior— conduct based on no ethics, value-neutral conduct, and value-based ethical conduct—and maintains that value-neutral conduct reflects "much of the present thinking in leading schools of contemporary public administration."[66] Value-free analysis may be an appropriate objective for social science research, but academic-based professional education must face ethical questions, address the principled analysis of public issues, and affirm acceptance of personal responsibility for the public trust.[67]

Stated differently, what is done with respect to the structural issues discussed in this study may be as important as the way they are accomplished.

Since public administration students, as students of organization, subject academic managerial efforts to special scrutiny, faculty need to be attentive to both the intended and unintended consequences of their actions.[68] Universities and their schools of public administration must demonstrate their own commitment to principled behavior by making a serious effort to deal with the ethical aspects of investment policies, employment practices, and other moral dilemmas in higher education.

Likewise, it should be recognized that much is learned by the example set in the daily conduct of the program. Thus condoning student and faculty dishonesty—widespread cheating and grade inflation—may teach behaviors that have functional equivalents in public administration such as credibility gaps and meaningless employee evaluations. While classroom ethical analysis can be an exciting intellectual endeavor to help place administration into its larger social context, to confine attention to formal courses may miss powerful opportunities for ethical reflection. Both structural components and proper environments for public administration programs must be available in professional education for the public service.

Students will be trying to define their identity and establish a level of integrity at which they will lead their professional lives. Brewster C. Denny believes that the academy, in the pursuit of the behavioral sciences, has forgotten how to teach intellectual rigor and the use of nonquantitative tools in writing, thinking, and recognizing the public interest.[69] If administrators are seen as being engaged in the art of managing, they are problem-solvers who must know how to ask and answer the right questions. American public administration was born as an instrument of good government. Since government is primarily concerned with values, schools of administration should be in the thick of the action through careful analysis of public issues.

To echo Rufus Miles, students should be encouraged to make a life-long habit of looking at problems from an increasingly broad point of view and from multiple perspectives.[70] The higher they move in the organizational hierarchy, the more they will encounter questions of social purpose. If they have a well-thought-out philosophy, their capacity for contributing to the definition of societal goals will be greater than it would otherwise be. Civil servants help shape policy not only by what they do, but also by what they are. Democratic government can effectively preside only if its employees serve as public servants and exemplars. If public administration is the "get-it-all-together profession,"[71] this surely is the ultimate task for educators in the field.

The affirmative attitude of the faculty toward encouraging young men and women with leadership potential to sharpen their sense of purpose is far more important than any single organizational technique or program structure. Education for and practice of public administration are normative to the core; public life without a concept of public service is hollow. Louis C. Gawthrop has correctly pointed out that if responsibility and responsiveness in American government have been sorely tested and found wanting in recent years, the role of bureaucracy in a democratic society appears to be the only question worthy of pursuit in the multistructured forms of public service education today.[72]

Notes

1. Carroll, J. D. Education for the Public Trust: Learning to Live with the Public and the Absurd. *The Bureaucrat 4* (April, 1975):24–25.
2. Frederickson, H. G. Public Administration in the 1970s. Developments and Directions. *Public Administration Review 36* (September/October, 1976):564–576.
3. Cited in Birkhead, G. S. and Carroll, J. D. Forward, in Birkhead, G. S. and Carroll, J. D. (eds.), *Education for Public Service 1979*, Maxwell School of Citizenship and Public Affairs, Syracuse University, Syracuse, N.Y., 1979, p. 6.
4. Moser, F. C. Introduction: the American setting, in Mosher, F. C. (ed.). *American Public Administration: Past, Present, Future.* University of Alabama Press, University, Alabama, 1975. See also Poore, D. M. The impact of NASPAA's standards on defining the field of public administration, in Uveges, J. A., Jr. (ed.). *Public Administration: History and Theory in Contemporary Perspective.* Marcel Dekker, Inc., New York, 1981: 85–104.
5. Golembiewski, R. T. The Near-Future of Graduate Public Administration in the U.S.: Some Program Minima, Their Common Violation, and Some Priority Palliatives. *Southern Review of Public Administration 3* (December 1979):323–359. Golembiewski and Mosher (n.4) maintain that the much discussed "turbulence" and identity crisis in public administration may not be as serious and important as some would have us believe, if for no other reason than many other disciplines are undergoing similar kinds of trauma.
6. Fritschler, A. L. and Mackelprang, A. J. Graduate Education in Public Affairs/Public Administration: Results of the 1975 Survey. *Public Administration Review 37* (September/October 1977):491.
7. An updated, empirical study of the different types of programs is currently being prepared for the National Association of Schools of Public Affairs and Administration by J. W. Ellwood, Princeton University.

8. Waldo, D. Introduction: trends and issues in education of public administration, in Birkhead and Carroll (eds.), *Education for Public Service 1979*, p. 17 ff.

9. Golembiewski, The Near Future of Graduate Public Administration, pp. 343-346.

10. Green, R. T., Hamm, R. D., and Keller, L. F. Undergraduate Education in Public Administration: An Empirical Analysis of Five Models of Academic Programs. Paper presented at the Annual Conference of the American Society for Public Administration, San Francisco Hilton, San Francisco, Calif., April 14-16, 1980.

11. Gates, B. L. and Doubleday, J. A Question of Focus: The Future of Education for the Public Service. *American Behavioral Scientist 21* (July/August 1978):907-910.

12. Waldo, D. Education for public administration in the seventies" in Mosher (ed.), *American Public Administration*, p. 184.

13. Fritschler and Mackelprang. Graduate Education in Public Affairs/ Public Administration, p. 491.

14. Beam, D. R. Public Administration is Alive and Well—And Living in the White House. *Public Administration Review 38* (January/February 1978):72-77.

15. Gates and Doubleday. A Question of Focus, p. 898.

16. Schick, A. Coming Apart in Public Administration. *Maxwell Review 10* (Winter 1973-1974):13-24.

17. Gawthrop, L. C. The Political System and Public Service Education. *American Behavioral Scientist 21* (July/August 1978):917.

18. Mosher. Introduction: the American setting, op. cit.

19. Wilson, W. The Study of Administration. *Political Science Quarterly 2* (June 1887):197-222.

20. Bowman, J. S. Public Administration Without Ethics: The Legacy of the Politics-Administration Dichotomy. Paper presented at the Annual Meeting of the American Political Science Association, Washington Hilton Hotel, Washington, D.C., August 28-31, 1980. Portions of this section are excerpted from the paper cited.

21. Henry, N. *Public Administration and Public Affairs.* 2d ed. Prentice-Hall, Englewood Cliffs, N.J., 1979, p. 133.

22. Gawthrop. The Political System, p. 920.

23. Denhardt, R. B. On the Management of Public Service Education. *Southern Review of Public Administration 3* (December 1979):273-283.

24. Mosher. Introduction: the American setting, p. 162.

25. National Academy of Public Administration. *Watergate: Implications for Responsible Government.* Basic Books, New York, 1974.

26. Gates and Doubleday. A Question of Focus, p. 895.

27. Agranoff, R. Universities and the Public Service: Developments and Perspectives. *American Behavioral Scientist 21* (July/August 1978):801–828.

28. Henry, N. The relevance question, in Birkhead and Carroll (eds.), *Education for Public Service 1979*, p. 27.

29. In addition to the Henry study (n.28), the National Longitudinal Study of Political Science, Public Administration/Public Affairs Graduates (principal investigators: Jack Rabin, Thomas Vocino, Samuel Yeager) may yield some relevant data.

30. Gawthrop. The Political System, pp. 924–925.

31. Denny, B. C. Address to the Third National Conference on Teaching Public Administration. Evergreen State College, Olympia, Wash., May 30, 1980 (mimeographed).

32. Henry. The relevance question, p. 43.

33. Englebert, E. A. The Findings and Implications of a Survey of Standards and Accreditation for Educational Programs in Public Administration. *Public Administration Review 37* (September/October 1977):523.

34. Waldo. Introduction: trends and issues, p. 17.

35. In all areas of public administration, and especially in undergraduate institutions, the percentage of programs housed in NASPAA affiliate schools has been shown to be remarkably low. See Laudicina, E. V. Graduate and undergraduate programs in public administration: perspectives on new forms of integration, in Birkhead and Carroll (eds.), *Education for Public Service 1979*, pp. 127–138.

36. Golembiewski. The Near Future of Graduate Public Administration, pp. 343–346. See also Gates and Doubleday. A Question of Focus.

37. Green, Hamm, and Keller. Undergraduate Education in Public Administration.

38. Denhardt, R. B. Teaching Public Administration as a Vocation. *Proceedings of the Third National Conference on Teaching Public Administration*. Adams, Guy (ed.) Evergreen State College, Olympia, Wash., 1980:91.

39. Kraemer, K. L. and Perry, J. L. Camelot Revisited: Public Administration Education in a Generic School. *Proceedings of the Third National Conference on Teaching Public Administration*, pp. 227–240.

40. The Task Force of the Undergraduate Section of NASPAA is currently looking into the internal cohesiveness of the models of education.

41. Kerrigan, J. E. and Hinton, D. W. Knowledge and Skills Needs for Tomorrow's Public Administrators. *Public Administration Review 40* (September/October 1980):460–473.

42. Plant, Jeremy F. Undergraduate Programs in Public Administration: Feeders, Familiarizers, Facilitators. Paper presented at the Annual Meeting of the National Association of Schools of Public Affairs/

Administration, Palacio del Rio Hilton Hotel, San Antonio, Tex., October 20, 1980.

43. Burgess, P. M. Capacity Buildings and the Elements of Public Management. *Public Administration Review 35* (December 1975):705–716.

44. Van Riper, P. P. Hit 'em Harder, John Hit 'em Harder. *Public Administration Review 27* (November 1967):339–342.

45. Golembiewski. The Near Future of Graduate Public Administration, p. 328.

46. National Association of Schools of Public Affairs/Administration. Guidelines and Standards for Professional Masters Degree Programs in Public Affairs/Public Administration. NASPAA, Washington, D.C., 1974.

47. Thayer, F. C. The NASPAA Threat. *Public Administration Review 36* (January/February 1976):85–90.

48. Bonser, C. F. A Response to the "NASPAA Threat." *Public Administration Review 36* (March/April 1976):250–251.

49. National Association of Schools of Public Affairs/Administration. *1980 Directory of Programs in Public Affairs and Administration.* NASPAA, Washington, 1980.

50. National Association of Schools of Public Affairs/Administration, reference (46):7–10.

51. Waldo. Introduction: trends and issues, p. 17.

52. Appleby, P. H. *Big Democracy.* Alfred A. Knopf, Inc., New York, 1945.

53. Schott, R. L. Public Administration as a Profession: Problems and Prospects. *Public Administration Review 36* (May/June 1970):253–259.

54. Fritschler and Mackelprang. Graduate Education in Public Affairs/Public Administration, p. 489.

55. Bowman, J. S. Managerial Theory and Practice of the Transfer of knowledge in Public Administration. *Public Administration Review 38* (November/December 1978):563–570.

56. Englebert, E. A. University Education for Public Policy Analysis. *Public Administration Review 37* (May/June 1977):228–235.

57. Nagel, S. and Neef, M. What Is and Should Be in University Policy Studies? *Public Administration Review 37* (July/August 1977):383–390.

58. Wilson. The Study of Administration.

59. Denhardt. On the Management of Public Service Education.

60. See Bowman, J. S. Teaching ethics in public administration, in Rizzo, A. and Heimovics, R. (eds.), *Innovations in Teaching Public Affairs/Administration*, Teaching Public Administration Conference, Kansas City/Miami, 1981:79–90.

61. Boling, T. E. Organizational ethics: rules, creativity, and idealism, in Sutherland, J. W. (ed.), *Management Handbook for Public Administration*, Van Nostrand Reinhold Co., New York, 1978:242, esp.

62. Bowman, J. S. Ethics in the Federal Service: A Post-Watergate View. *Midwest Review of Public Administration 11* (March 1977):3-21.

63. See, e.g., Boling. Organization Ethics.

64. Phillips, S. Educating the public servant, in Birkhead and Carroll (eds.). *Education for Public Service 1979*, pp. 77-89.

65. Agranoff. Universities and the Public Service.

66. Gordon, P. Ethics and the Public Service—Recommendations for the Training of Public Servants. Paper presented to the Directors and Staff of the Bureau of Training and the General Management Training Center, U.S. Civil Service Commission, February 22, 1977:4.

67. Denny. Address to the Third National Conference on Teaching Public Administration.

68. Denhardt. On the Management of Public Service Education.

69. Denny. Address to the Third National Conference on Teaching Public Administration.

70. Miles, R. E., Jr. The Search for Identity of Graduate Schools of Public Affairs. *Public Administration Review 27* (November 1967):347.

71. Cleveland, H. The Get-It-All-Together Profession. *Public Administration Review 39* (July/August 1979):306-309.

72. Gawthrop. The Political System, p. 919.

6
Adult Learning Methods in Public Administration Education

Deborah J. Young* and William B. Eddy
University of Missouri, Kansas City, Missouri

Many students in academic public administration programs are adults. Many
are also nontraditional in other ways, that is, they work full time, they are
pursuing careers, and they have family and community obligations. What are
faculty members in public administration programs doing to respond to these
nontraditional adult students? Are concepts from the fields of adult education and management development having an impact in the classroom, or are
instructional approaches from undergraduate social science disciplines still
holding sway? What educational techniques are available to faculty members
and what choices are there to make about the design and management of
offerings?

This review will explore the preceding questions with emphasis on what is
currently taking place in colleges and universities as reported in the literature.
We will omit from direct emphasis several obviously important, related
topics, including career development, internships and noncredit continuing

Present affiliation: Training and Career Development, General Services
Administration, Kansas City, Missouri.

education. Each of these will come into the discussion, but our major interest is in the pertinence of adult education concepts to the classroom.

Frank Sherwood has observed that, "Public Administration has emerged as a discipline because of its enrollment of part-time, in career students."[1] Yet it was in the early 1970s before consciousness about the implications of adult learners began to grow. The Federal Executive Institute was established in 1968 and drew heavily on the work of pioneer adult educator Malcolm Knowles as well as related applied behavioral science training methods.[2] The format emphasized diagnosis of learning needs, the relating of personal self-awareness to professional development, participative training designs, and the careful building of a learning climate. The early 1970s also saw the establishment of the National Training and Development Service, the Academy of Professional Development of the International City Management Association, the Intergovernmental Personnel Act, and other major programs to stimulate the learning and development of adults in public sector careers.

Frank Sherwood's presidential address to the 1973 American Society for Public Administration annual conference took adult continuing education as a major theme. Later that year a symposium in the *Public Administration Review* edited by Tom Fletcher provided the first significant infusion of the topic into the public management literature.[3] (We make that statement because none of the seven symposium papers contains a reference to a writing on adult education as it relates to public administration.) Fred Fisher sounded the theme in the first paper, entitled "Give a Damn About Adult Continuing Education," in which he affirmed the need for public managers to stay involved in learning activities throughout their careers. Other articles by McGill, Donaldson, Collins, Shaw, and Gregg and Van Maanen explored methods for adults engaged in administrative careers in the public service to continue their learning. Some discussed educational methods and philosophies. Collins, for example, foresaw the increasing emphasis on individual needs and feelings (which he referred to as organization development) and voiced concern about its tendency to divert energy from the need for public and private responsibility.

It appears that the awareness of the needs and techniques of adult education in agency and professional training and development activities was slightly ahead of the awareness of the same issues on many campuses. The report of the 1975 National Association of Schools of Public Affairs and Administration (NASPAA) did not discuss such factors as the ages of students enrolled in member schools, nor did it mention the various innovative approaches to teaching and class scheduling which were beginning to be tried.[4] This was in spite of the fact that many campuses were offering evening courses and a few, including the Universities of Oklahoma and Southern

California, were providing instruction in concentrated time blocks over week-ends. No doubt, many faculty members were also using teaching methods which departed from the traditional lecture-discussion methods and included exercises, simulations and independent projects. In 1975 Dwight Waldo mentioned an increasing emphasis on adult education as well as criticism of the formality and rigidity of traditional education.[5]

Another impetus to the consideration of alternative teaching methods was the publication in 1974 of the *Guidelines and Standards* for the member schools of the National Association of Schools of Public Administration and Affairs.[6] These guidelines not only prescribed the substantive areas that should be covered in academic degree programs, but spoke to the need for the development of skills and competencies of performance as well as the acquisition of knowledge. This stance served to remind faculty members of the professional nature of public administration education connoting a need to devise "hands-on" learning for skill development in contrast to the more traditional academic programs in fields such as political science.

This chapter will explore adult education methods in public administration. Before doing that, however, we will look briefly at the field of adult education.

The Adult Education Movement

In his book *The Adult Education Movement in the U.S.* Malcolm Knowles chronicles the development of the adult education movement from colonial times up to the present decade.[7]

Between the years 1600 and 1779 education in the United States was primarily aimed toward a liberal, utilitarian, secular concept, as opposed to the European tradition of class structure and theological orthodoxies. Between 1780 and 1865 the idea that adults, as well as children, need education was noted. Three permanent institutional forms of adult education began, these being the local institute or adult school (only in a few large cities), the library, and the museum. The adult evening school was just beginning to develop as the fourth major institutional form. From 1866 through 1920 correspondence schools, summer schools, and university extension divisions were established. With the development of these new institutional forms came new methods of teaching, such as the demonstration method pioneered by the Cooperative Extension Service, the home study course, and the short-term institute. There was increased government involvement as evidenced by the creation of the Department of Education, the Smith-Lever Act creating the Cooperative Extension Service, and the passage of the Smith Hughes

Vocational Education Act. In the years between 1921 and 1961, adult education became an integral part of the American way of life. Whereas before 1920 the term "adult education" did not appear even in the professional educational vocabulary, by 1960 this term was widely used as a symbol of a significant aspect of the national institutional system. An adult education field was beginning to take shape.

Three organizations contributing substantially to the development of a sense of cohesion and professionalism in the field were developed between 1924 and 1961. These were the American Association for Adult Education, the National Education Association Department of Adult Education, and the Adult Education Association. From 1961 until the present the field of adult education has continued to expand, with many youth-serving institutions becoming adult-serving. The educational level of adult students has continued to rise, and the resources and facilities to educate them are gradually expanding. There has been a rapid expansion in the body of knowledge about the education of adults.

A number of scholars have contributed to the understanding and definition of the field of adult education. Among them are Cyrus O. Houle, Allen Tough, Malcolm Knowles, and David A. Kolb. Before Cyrus O. Houle began his investigation in the 1950s, research had been aimed at describing the behavior of adults, i.e., who studies what, where, and when. Houle gave impetus to examining the psychology of adult education; that is, what motivates the adult to study?[8] These studies have been extended by Allen Tough at the Ontario Institute for Studies in Education. Tough has branched out, looking at the adult learner in situations other than the organized classroom setting. He is also concerned with how adults learn and what help they obtain in order to learn. He defines learning "projects" and the three overlapping categories of learners: (1) goal oriented, (2) activity oriented, and (3) learning oriented. Among the many who were influenced by Houle is Malcolm Knowles. Knowles has concentrated on the importance of the learning climate. He identifies learning goals for adults and designs learning activities—models around which other adult educators can design their courses. Originally Knowles organized his ideas around the concept of informal adult education. Then, in the mid-sixties he adopted the term *andragogy*. Using this as an organizing concept, he argues that as an individual matures, he or she develops the capacity to be self-directing, to utilize his or her own readiness to learn, and to organize learning around life problems.[9] The traditional term *pedagogy* refers, in its Greek root, to teaching children. Andragogy denotes adults as learners.

David A. Kolb, along with Irwin M. Rubin and James M. McIntyre, developed *Organizational Psychology, an Experiential Approach,*[10] the first widely used work which provided instructors in organizational behavior with material for the experience-based learning process. Kolb's "Experiential Learning Model" emphasizes the important role that experience plays in the learning process, an emphasis that differentiates this approach from other cognitive learning theories. There are two goals in the experiential learning process; one is to learn the specifics of a particular subject matter, and the other is to learn about one's own strengths and weaknesses as a learner, that is, learning how to learn from experience.[11] This model has led us to think in terms of experiental techniques to meet the needs of adult learners.

In 1975 *Exchange: The Organizational Behavior Teaching Journal* was established. Although oriented toward MBA programs, it is also read by public administration faculty members and has become a primary resource for ideas about nontraditional teaching in management.[12] The three national conferences on the teaching of public administration have also contributed to the available literature.

Adults in Public Administration Programs

In order to gain an up-to-date picture of the status of nontraditional teaching situations in public administration programs, a brief questionnaire was mailed to the directors of all NASPAA member programs. The questionnaire inquired about age, career status, and course loads of both undergraduate and graduate students as well as for indications of programmatic measures to respond to in-career students. One hundred fourteen questionnaires were returned, about half of the total membership of NASPAA.

To obtain the proportion of "adult" students in the programs, we asked respondents for the percentage of their graduate students 25 years of age or older. Twenty-five is an arbitrary cutoff point which we believed would exclude most traditional precareer students who had gone straight into graduate programs after completing baccalaureate degrees. We are defining adult students not in terms of voting majority, but with regard to the fact that they do not fit the typical continuing student category and thus may have different experiences and needs. Figure 1 shows the distribution of students over 25 by percentage categories. It is evident that in the majority of graduate programs half or more of the students fit into our category of adult students.

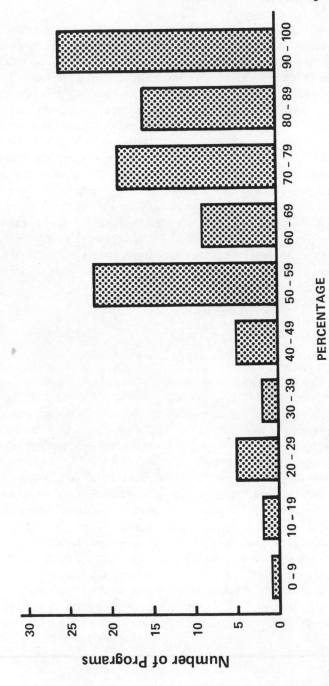

Figure 1   Percentage of graduate students in public administration programs 25 years of age or older.

The distribution of adult undergraduate students (not shown graphically in this paper) was very much the opposite of the graduate data. Only 11 programs out of the 46 reporting showed 50 percent or more of their students over 25, whereas 29 programs indicated 20 percent or less were over 25.

Figure 2 shows the percentage of graduate students who are "in-career", which we defined as "working in a career-oriented job beyond the beginning entry level." It is clear from the findings that a high proportion of the students in the responding programs are in-career. Seventy programs report that 50 percent or more of their students fit the in-career category. The median proportion falls in the 60 to 69 percent interval.

Again the distribution of undergraduate students is the opposite. Only 6 programs report 50 percent or more in-career students and 29 indicate less than 20 percent.

The third question asked for the proportion of students who are part-time (carrying less than a full academic course load). Figure 3 shows the distribution. A very large majority of the programs (76) report 50 percent or more of their students are part-time. This appears to be an increase over the results of the 1975 NASPAA Survey,[13] although the data in the two studies are not fully comparable. (Again, the distribution of part-time students among undergraduates is the opposite, with few programs reporting a substantial proportion of undergraduate public administration students.)

Thus, it is clear from an inspection of the survey results that the vast majority of faculty members who teach in graduate programs in public administration are dealing with nontraditional students, a clientele unlike those for whom standard classroom lecture-discussion methods were developed. The typical graduate student in public administration is over 25, has had professionally oriented work experience and attends part time. Replies to the final question, which asked for programmatic responses to adult students, will be dealt with later in the chapter.

A search for materials regarding adult education methods in public administration programs provided a modest number of published articles. It appears that the topic has not attained the popularity or status to achieve a significant inroad into the academic and professional literature. In an attempt to locate more material, including conference presentations and unpublished pieces, we sent letters to NASPAA program directors which we asked be circulated to their faculties. The letters requested references on the topic. Much of the discussion that follows is based on the material sent us, plus the Proceedings of the Public Administration Teaching Conferences held in 1978, 1979, and 1980. Many papers report the experiences of a single educational program and its response to a problem or area of need.

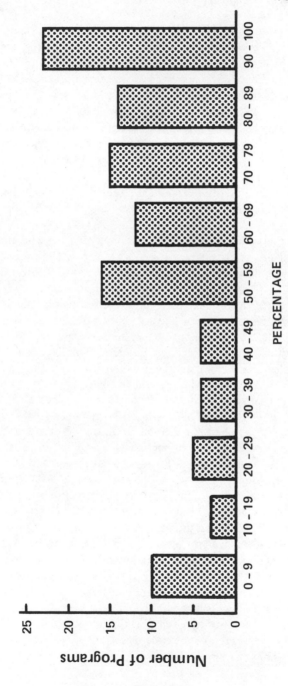

Figure 2 Percentage of "in-career" graduate students in public administration programs.

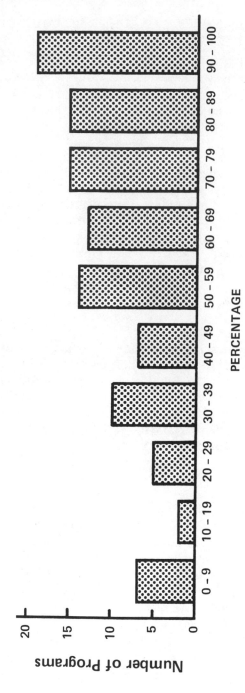

Figure 3 Percentage of part-time graduate students in public administration programs.

The adult education activities in public administration programs divide themselves into the following categories, which serve to organize our discussion:

1. Delivery systems: Accomodating the realities of adult students' lives through nontraditional class times, locations, or schedules.
2. Methodology: The use of teaching techniques that depart from traditional lecture-discussion methods, including experience-based designs, self-directed learning, and various uses of small groups.
3. Response to students' needs: Techniques for need diagnosis, structuring learning around needs, and helping students deal with life issues.
4. Classroom management, philosophy, and style: Approaches to sharing among faculty and students the responsibilities for class content and procedures.
5. Skill development: Approaches to emphasizing the performance and competency aspects of education rather than concentrating solely on theory and information.

Delivery Systems

Probably the most evident manifestations of the need to deal with nontraditional students are classes schedules at times and in places to accomodate attendance by working adults. Paige[14] reports a study of students' attitudes regarding part-time public administration programs at the University of San Francisco. Among reasons for selecting the USF program, convenience of time when classes are offered was most often listed. Location of the program and the fact that it is geared for working adults were also listed among the top five reasons. Similar findings in formal and informal surveys at other universities have undoubtedly accounted for the surge in nontraditional delivery systems.

For many years academic courses in public administration have been offered in the evening. Such schedule changes in themselves have probably required relatively little modification in teaching technique. But the newer designs involving concentrated blocks of time during weekend periods have required rethinking of approaches to course planning. The University of Oklahoma, University of Southern California, and Nova University were among the pioneers in the model labelled by Neely Gardner the "intensive semester."[15] Those who report on intensive-semester projects describe some of the challenges and problems of mounting such offerings.

Several universities, the leader probably being the University of Oklahoma, offer public administration degrees at many off-campus locations—some in remote foreign locations. Heise[16] describes a newer program developed by Florida International University and offered "far from hearth and home" to Mexican government employees at an off-site location. In an attractive residential retreat setting, faculty meet with students for eight-day seminars which are preceded by eight-week periods of independent study and preparation. In addition to the usual problems of library resources, admission procedures and advising, the need for bridging language and cultural differences provides a special challenge. Study guides and resource materials are prepared, and simultaneous translations of classroom lectures and discussions are provided. The author concludes that the most effective safeguard to assure that the courses are relevant to the realities of Mexican public administration is the experienced mid-career status of the students, which allows them to scrutinize much more effectively the body of knowledge presented, to test it carefully, and the accept only that which is adaptable to their own situations.

Another educational delivery system involves taking courses off campus to the employing agency of the students. Figliola[17] describes a collaborative arrangement between Long Island University and Nassau and Suffolk Counties. Classes meet at county facilities in order to reduce travel time and cost and are offered during evenings or weekends or at 7:30 a.m. This type of arrangement provides public agencies an opportunity to upgrade skills of their professional personnel within the constraints of limited resources and time demands.

The College of the Virgin Islands[18] has developed a management intern program in collaboration with the Virgin Islands government which provides even closer integration of the classroom experience and the agency's manpower needs. This program is an example of a highly developed extended delivery system. Students selected for this program are rotated through specific work assignments based on individual development plans established early in the program. The program is jointly coordinated between the college and the government and culminates in a permanent position for the student, who must sign an agreement to stay with the government for twice the length of the intern program.

Two papers describe the problems and opportunities involved in delivering graduate degrees through off-campus centers. Wessel[19] describes the efforts of Iowa State, a university not located in a larger metropolitan area, to respond to declining enrollment by seeking new student clientele through geographical decentralization. Six sites located from 90 to 190 miles from the

central campus deliver MPA coursework to in-career students. An evaluation
of the program revealed that students found one of the significant benefits
to be the opportunity to associate with other public employees and discuss
their work experiences. Also, the decentralized system proved to be of
benefit to a significant number of students who moved around the state because of work mobility, but were still able to pursue their degrees.

Ohio University delivers programs through five off-campus sites, most in
economically underdeveloped areas of Appalachia. Weinberg[20] describes the
problems and strategies attendant on such programs. In addition to the usual
off-campus problems with libraries, computers, advising, and the many layers
of the university bureaucracy which seem always to delay attempts to inno-
vate, there are some unique issues. These include the traditional bias against
"applied education" within political science departments, the need for off-
campus centers to maintain fiscal self-sufficiency (in contrast to the more
heavily subsidized main campus program), and the more rural and homoge-
neous student bodies. An additional problem is the supervision of local
practitioners who function as adjunct faculty at the off-campus sites. One
of the interesting outcomes was the development of a special curriculum in
rural and small community administration which was better suited to the
needs and realities of the off-campus students than was the more cosmopoli-
tan focus of the main campus MPA program. The author also observes that
the off-campus in-career students are more demanding than on-campus
students.

Giallourakis[21] describes an innovative program at the University of
Wisconsin-Oshkosh designed to deliver off-campus courses to in-career students. The core curriculum consists of 12 self-paced modules each worth
1 hour of credit. Students work on the modules independently at their homes
or offices. Each is designed specifically for the program and supervised by a
faculty member through meetings throughout the state and by telephone.
The 12 to 18 hour "professional emphasis" is made up of regular graduate
courses from the University at Oshkosh or another institution in the University of Wisconsin system closer to the student's home. A final seminar consists of a field research project on a problem of interest to the student.

The system for assigning faculty resources to the program at Oshkosh is
also innovative. There are no permanent faculty assigned to the program,
except for the director. Staffing is contracted for with several academic
departments—an arrangement called "matrix staffing." Grants and released
time are provided for course development. Studies indicate that after the
modules are developed, time invested is comparable with traditional courses.

The difference is that the instructor "function(s) as a resource person rather than a lecturing machine."

Additional information about course delivery is provided by the questionnaires (see p. 59) which we mailed to NASPAA member programs. We asked, "If you have adult in-career students in your program, do you do anything to respond to them differently than you respond to traditional students?" Seventy-nine offer courses during the evening, six mentioned late afternoon classes, two hold lunch-time classes, and nineteen offer courses on weekends. Thirteen offer courses off-campus. A number of schools mentioned support services adapted to adults' needs—evening and off-campus registration and advising, for example.

A final issue to be mentioned under the rubric of delivery systems is the offering of graduate credit for what is often referred to as "life experience," a category of postlearning opportunities which may include work experience, training, and noncredit education. The Ohio University program described above grants credit for certain kinds of on-the-job projects, as do several other graduate programs in public administration.[22] This trend has come about because of the increasing number of in-career adults entering graduate programs with work experience which provides competency in the same substantive areas covered by course work. There are several important issues involved in the topic. The first is largely philosophical and deals with the question of whether degrees ought to be granted in part on the basis of "real-life" experience rather than formal academic course work. If the answer is affirmative, the next problem is how to acquire a defensible and reliable method of assessing the amount of credit due for a given experience. Laudicina[23] discusses several criteria. The first is that it is *learning* rather than simply experience which provides the basis for credit, and it is the learning which should be assessed. Some schools, including Kean College, provide credit only for experiences which correspond to courses actually listed in the catalog. Under this system the request for credit is evaluated by the instructor for that course. The other approach, more often used by external degree "colleges without walls" is based on the question of whether the experience provided learning at the college level. Three methods of assessment have been developed. These are: portfolio documentation (job performance data, work samples, testimony from supervisors), written or oral examinations, and performance demonstrations. Under any evaluation system a clear statement of the competency standards and evaluation methods should be agreed to prior to application. There appears to be a lack of consensus in the field about the acceptability of granting credit for life experience, but it is clearly an area that will draw increasing pressure as the proportion of students with relevant work experience increases.

Methodology

Current methods for providing adult educational experiences vary from informal discussions or case presentations to complex simulations running for a full semester. The preferred approach would not be to choose a method based on its appeal and simply adapt course material to it, but rather to design the course, drawing on whatever methods are most appropriate for the materials, the students, the situation, the instructor's skills, and so forth. Eddy proposes a model based on Knowles's concepts. It involves (1) goal definition, (2) climate setting, (3) need diagnosis, (4) contracting, (5) resource identification and affirmation, (6) implementing experiential techniques, and (7) evaluation. Experiential methods available include questionnaires, discussion, delphi and nominal group techniques, simulations, consulting pairs or trios, plays as cases, and demonstrations.[24] A major consideration for an instructor who undertakes implementation of experiential techniques is that he or she should be comfortable with and confident in the technique, lest these uncertainties be transmitted to the students.

Brown identifies three types of experiential learning: Type I or "How to" learning, Type II or "Role Socialization", and Type II or "Autonomous Use of Experience for Learning."[25] Each of these addresses a different set of goals in a professional education program and therefore requires different approaches to experiential learning. Type I involves going through a carefully constructed experience in order to learn a specific concept or skill (for example, learning to interview). In Type II the learner experiences the world of the practitioner (as in an internship). Type II requires that the student be an active participant in the learning process but that he or she become an active learner with an influential role in structuring the learning process.

Wolf suggests that it is not a question of either traditional classroom or experiential learning, rather the challenge is to invent ways to use both approaches to complete the learning cycle and to help students in their effort to learn from their experience.[26] He mentions several approaches to experiential learning used at the Washington Public Affairs Center of the University of Southern California, which require few decisions and materials, demand less start-up time and costs, and involve less prior faculty skill development. The internship is the oldest and most widely used format. The USC School of Public Administration offers an MPA degree in intergovernment

management. As part of the program, students spend a semester in Los
Angeles, Sacramento, and Washington, D.C. In each location they take
courses and complete an internship during which they write a review of what
they learned. Supervisors write a letter evaluating each intern's performance,
based on a working/learning agreement. This letter is considered in the final
grade. The administrative journal is mentioned as an experiential tool.

A number of more structured experiential tools have been used in the
professional public administration program at the University of Southern
California. One of these is the application paper in which students are expected to relate explicitly conceptual material from the courses to a practice
environment. At the USC Washington Public Affairs Center students complete an independent field research project as part of their requirements.
Students select an area of interest that involves some issue of public administration dealing with the particular course focus, and interview 8 to 10 knowledgeable people. Field visits, briefings, and short papers link specific observations about the visits to readings and lectures.

An experiential approach is used to teach MPA students at the Capitol
Campus of Pennsylvania State University who are employed full-time in various public and nonprofit agencies.[27] The concern is to bridge the gap between the real world and existing theory and research. An organization
behavior course is operated from the viewpoint that the class is a functioning
social system, a miniorganization, and that attention is paid to the impact of
the learning *process* as well as *what* is to be learned. An attempt is made to
establish individual responsibility for learning among class members by developing individual learning goals, plans, and required resources. Class meetings
are based upon design principles of experiential learning (the work of Harrison
and Hopkins[28] and Kolb[29]) and include exercises designed to have members
experience some of the key processes and dynamics covered in the assigned
readings. Following the exercise, individuals discuss their experiences with
the instructor-facilitator. Special attention is given to developing effective
feedback mechanisms and encouraging individuals to develop the skills required to give and receive interpersonal feedback.

Evans, Hall, and Rinehart[30] acknowledge the characteristics of adult
learners as described by Knowles and indicate that there are three considerations for those who design, schedule, and teach public administration to
part-time adult learners. First, instructors must use materials that link theoretical, conceptual, and methodological points to the students' administrative
experiences in public organizations. Second, instructors must employ interactive teaching methods and techniques that allow students to work together
in groups to the maximum extent possible. Third, the format of the course/

workshop must be such that the schedule of the class does not impede the
formation, maturation, and problem-solving capabilities of student groups or
the instructor's ability to utilize proper materials and "coaching." Because
of these considerations the authors recommend the following approach
exemplified in the master's degree program in public administration at
Russell Sage College in Albany, New York: (1) Classes and training sessions
must be scheduled in at least four-hour blocks, preferably away from the
workplace. (2) Such classes and training sessions of more than fifteen participants should be team taught. (3) Instructors should facilitate the formation
of groups and involve the students in learning from each other. (4) Materials
should be relevant to the students' work and career plans. (5) Finally, students must participate and learn by doing.

Changes in the view of public personnel management and changes in American higher education have resulted in new techniques appropriate for teaching public personnel management. Klingner indicates that case studies and
simulations emphasize the evaluative or public policy implications of public
personnel, offering students a chance to study the contradictions and compromises which make up public policy.[31] Consultation or community service
projects arranged for students to obtain academic credit are a means of ac-
quainting students with the structure and methods of a project work team,
and with the realities of seeking to understand and influence the client organization's activities. Mid-career students can be encouraged to use their access
to work organizations to gather data for research in support of hypotheses
about comparative effectiveness of personnel techniques. Klingner also suggests that these teaching-learning techniques are relevant to other administrative areas as well as to public personnel management.

Responding to Students' Needs

In traditional university education the emphasis has been almost exclusively
on the subject matter or content, with little focus on the student and his or
her needs as a person. Perhaps it is only a slight exaggeration to assert that
students have been viewed largely as vessels which sit passively as they are
filled up with knowledge. Although there may be long-term payoffs promised ("You'll need to know this when you get out on the job.") or a claim
that discipline is good for you (à la Professor Kingsford of *Paperchase*), the
substantive field has traditionally dominated. This trend has begun to change
a little under the influence of androgogy, experienced-based learning designs
and other related viewpoints from consulting and counseling. It is now

becoming slightly more common to weave student self-diagnosis into the course format, to leave room in the syllabus for some things the students want to learn, and to assist students with life and career planning. Many of the papers reviewed in this chapter discuss approaches to addressing students' learning needs and life situations. See particularly Eddy,[32] Skruber and Rizzo,[33] and Denhardt.[34] Also see Figliola for an example of a needs study.[35]

A general approach, which stems from Knowles's and others' recommendations for adult education, begins with a broadly defined purpose for a given course and provides an early opportunity to students to identify their own learning needs and interests within the parameters. Thus, students may select subtopics from the broader field, pursue individual projects which help them learn how to apply the knowledge they gain to a particular problem area, or work in groups with similar interests to help each other gain skill or proficiency. This approach is based on the assumption that adult students know what they need to learn, can contribute a good deal to the learning process, will be more motivated to learn if they are pursuing objectives which are personally meaningful, and a classroom which takes students' learning interests into account provides a climate which is more conducive to learning.

Other views of the learning experience perceive the relevant sphere of student needs more broadly than simply *learning* needs. These views emphasize the importance of dealing with the whole person in the educational process—not just his or her learning needs or cognitive abilities. The assumption is that the student as a total human being is the appropriate level of concern. The student's career progress, life context, relationships, motivations, and other personal factors are very much with him or her in the classroom and need to be taken into account in the educational process.

One approach to dealing with the individual in the educational experience is the self assessment/career planning course in the University of Southern California Doctor of Public Administration Program.[36] A variety of exercises and experiences are used to help students understand themselves better and make informed career and educational choices. These include an extensive autobiography, self-assessment questionnaires and interviews, a life planning exercise, and feedback from tohers. The course culminates with the formulation of a self-development/learning plan which provides a blueprint for future learning activities, including DPA (Doctor of Public Administration) courses. The author belives that the self-assessment/career planning course, by better relating the educational experience to students' needs, increases student motivation to participate in and complete the program.

Mocker and Spear warn against the assumption that any inquiry about what a student wants constitutes a valid needs assessment.[37] They caution that one cannot assume that responses to abstract questions are indicators of motivation. The authors introduce a conceptual framework for understanding alternative approaches to needs assessment. Surveys may be descriptive of one's own needs or prescriptive in regard to what others should learn; they may also be either subjective or objective. A variety of assessment methods are available for a given set of circumstances.

Classroom Management and Participation

The university classroom has traditionally been a bastion of authoritarian management. The professor, with legitimate expert power, attested to by credentials and backed up by the bureaucracy and traditions of the academy, reigns supreme. Learning objectives, substance, grading and teaching methods are determined unilaterally by the faculty. Adult educators and management theorists have begun to question this model on several grounds, at least as it applies to public administration education. One issue is that such an approach probably does not establish a climate that is most conducive to learning. It fosters short-term memorization rather than integration. Another problem is that the autocratic classroom does not provide a very good management model for students, since such unilateral methods are usually neither applicable nor effective in the "real world." Still another issue identified by Denhardt and Kirkhart[38] is that the authority-based classroom derives largely from the positivist view of science, which artifically separates fact from values and feelings and stresses the expert's preconceived realities rather than helping the student learn to understand the situation via his or her own realities. This distinction has, of course, major implications for the applicability of theory.

Denhardt and Kirkhart propose a model for classroom education which attempts to cope with some of the above problems. Their seven-stage developmental cycle involves: (1) building a supportive learning climate, (2) structuring mutual planning, (3) needs assessment, (4) joint formulation of educational objectives, (5) organizing and staffing the learning community (classroom) to match objectives and resources, (6) implementation, and (7) results diagnosis. This approach is aimed at not only coping with the weaknesses of traditional instruction but also provides a better format for learning and understanding the increasingly changing and turbulent environment of the public sector.

Skruber and Rizzo discuss another facet of what they refer to as "democracy in the classroom", that of evaluation. Traditionally, faculty-dominated evaluation systems not only reinforce dependency but also shift students away from working to meet their own needs. This lowers their stake in the learning process, encourages memorization rather than higher-level understanding, and makes the grade the major objective.

The authors contend that a primary goal of education is teaching individuals *how to learn*, that is, "the ability to assess and identify which skills and knowledge are important for their own development, which learning methods shall be employed and how they shall assess their own performance." They propose a teacher-student shared authority model for learning and evaluation which they call *student certification*. In an application of student certification, a course is organized around a set of specifiable skills. These skills may be specified by the teacher or decided jointly with the students. The authors describe the process as follows:

> Once the skills to be learned have been determined, the students are organized into teams which are responsible for conducting one or more certification sessions. Under the guidance of the teacher, the teams are responsible for researching literature pertinent to the skill, operationalizing the skill into specific criteria of performance, designing a certification activity, and conducting a certification class session. When this work is complete, the teacher uses the process that the certification team has designed to certify the students composing the certification team so that they become expert in the skill. After being certified in the skill themselves, the certification teams are then authorized to certify others in the skill.[39]

The authors admit that there are a number of unsolved problems inherent in the transfer of authority through student certification. These include the time and energy required for group consultation, the dramatic change in the instructor's role and (for some) the accompanying anxiety, and the difficulty of adapting some courses to the model. Nevertheless, they deem the technique worth pursuing because the learning appears to be more concrete and lasting and both students and instructor enjoy learning more.

Denhardt[40] has broadened the focus of the issues we have discussed in this section to apply them to the management of overall public service education programs. It is his assertion that the style in which program directors respond to the various issues of personnel, resources, and procedures affects the character and the learning style of the programs. The contrasting traditions of instrumental-efficiency and normative-educative approaches provide choice

points regarding how to deal with problems and communicate to students
models of administrative behavior. The normative tradition in public administration urges managers to represent the best qualities of a democratic
society—freedom, justice, equality, and personal responsibility. It is Denhardt's view that if these qualities prevail in the management of public
administration programs, a more supportive, need-oriented, and responsible
learning community will evolve.

Theory versus Skill

In-career students desire an education that will assist them to reach their
career potential by the most direct path. There is controversy as to what is
the ideal curriculum for such an education in the field of public administration. There are those who believe that theory alone is worthy of academic
endeavor and that if one understands the theory, application on the job will
follow naturally. Others contend that today's occupational opportunities
demand specific skills which need to be directly addressed in the classroom.
Still others advocate a carefully orchestrated combination of theory and
practice. Orion White has suggested the term *praxis* to connote the integration of theory and practice and the rejection of the traditional dichotomy of
academic and practitioner.[41]

Jreisat[42] views theory as an essential part of teaching public administration.
The crucial test of any administrative theory is the capacity to guide action
in useful ways. "To evaluate the usefulness of educational programs in terms
of immediate applicability to jobs would deprive students of the full range of
benefits (verbal ability, broad and general information, alternative ways of
looking at the world) usually derived from university education." "On the
other hand," Jreisat continues, "overemphasis of the academic or theoretical
dimension in some programs must be examined. The abstract approach to
teaching this field suffers a narrowness and incompleteness similar to that of
the nuts-and-bolts approach." Balance of emphasis is critical.

Eddy describes a course entitled Group Behavior[43] which illustrates some
approaches to teaching operational skills. The purposes are to help students
learn principles of group dynamics and team effectiveness, while helping
them to evaluate and increase their skills in interpersonal and group situations.
Students are formed into functioning groups the first week of class. During
the early stages of the term there are specific assignments or structured tasks
or exercises. As the term progresses, there are fewer structured assignments
and fewer intergroup sessions, as the groups develop their own autonomy

and momentum. No specific reading assignments are made, but students are told that the books will be helpful in understanding their group experiences. Journals are kept by students for recording experiences, reactions and learning in their groups. Short papers are assigned on topics such as "How I See My Group" or "My Learning Needs and Goals." The journals and short papers are vehicles for recording and analyzing behavior and relating it to theory. Cross-consulting pairs meet to discuss their contrasting experiences.

Some assumptions posed by Eddy about human learning in settings such as public administration education are as follows:

1. The learning of skill and the learning of knowledge are not incompatible; that is, one does not cancel out the other.
2. Knowledge may be gained through a single modality (reading or listening) but knowledge is gained more effectively and retained longer and more completely if multiple modalities are utilized (seeing, listening, discussing, analyzing, etc.).
3. The learning of skills in an academic-professional program requires all the elements of the learning of knowledge plus application, practice, and feedback.
4. Students need the most help from an expert, such as a faculty member, in locating sound and relevant sources of knowledge (reading materials, etc.). But, they can learn the material for themselves, without the professor's help (except for clearing up obscurities or misunderstandings).
5. The professor may influence students' motivation to learn by the classroom climate, rewards and punishments, and by the relevance of the learning to real-world application.
6. Students' motivation to learn knowledge is greatly enhanced if they need the knowledge as a foundation upon which to build application skills that are to be used and evaluated in important settings.

Zauderer and Ross[44] assert that academic institutions can achieve responsive educational programming if two conditions are met. The first is to create an organizational culture which encourages faculty to focus on the educational needs offstudents. The second condition relates to the quality of a curriculum as evidenced by making it responsive to the demands of the employment market place. The authors describe the Masters of Public Administration (MPA) program at the American University, using these two conditions as an organizing theme. An MPA task force evaluated the existing curriculum and formed conclusions upon which a new program was formed. This new program "encourages students to select courses in light of their educational needs and career interests, and is flexible enough to provide students with a greater measure of choice in course selection." Ross and Zauderer believe the most innovative additions to the curriculum are the skill modules. As described by them, each student selects two skill modules, designed to build competencies which are not often treated in traditional graduate courses. Many of the modules are taught by professionals who have established reputations in a specialized field. Students earn two credits for each module which includes 20 hours of instruction and are graded on a pass/fail basis.

The module on written communication focuses on the problems of style, grammar, content, and organization as they apply to government report writing, memos, letters, and so on. Two modules in budgeting provide students with an opportunity to simulate the budget process by working with forms and materials used at different levels of government. Other skill modules are meeting skills and managerial effectiveness, computer systems literacy, survey research for public affairs, and grant writing.

Toward effective integration of theory and practice in public administration, Greenhill, Metz, and Stander[45] describe a performance-based curricular approach consisting of substantive "Competence-Based Areas", that is, knowledge-based capabilities or CBAs. These are personal professional attributes which shape and characterize performance. The model includes CBA learning packages with operationally defined educational objectives, assessment criteria and materials, and a variety of supplementary educational resources. The following are examples of the CBA titles included in their "Theory/Practice Project Model": (1) understanding public agency structure and administrative processes, (2) implementing statutory programs and policies, and (3) communicating public agency policies, plans, and practices. The model further delineates the personal/professional attributes or "capacities" which characterize the performance envisioned in the CBAs. Assessment to determine the nature and extent of the program's impact on student learning is accomplished in a variety of ways including traditional methods (e.g., multiple-choice, true-false) as well as innovative techniques (e.g., role playing/simulations, rating sheets, and specially adapted professional formats). The authors believe their competence-based approach has important advantages for adult learners and their performance in public management settings. Mid-career students in particular have requested academic credit for prior learning; for example, for areas of expertise they claim to have developed in work settings. It is suggested that performance-based instruments, such as theirs, may be a promising approach toward assessing classroom-based and prior learning.

Conclusion

It seems clear from the literature that academic public administration is becoming a nontraditional educational field. Some of the forces influencing the change are demographic and logistic. They include the part-time, in-career student bodies, geographical dispersion, agency use of academic programs for management development, and adults returning to school. Other forces have to do with the increasing professionalization of the field and involve increasing legitimacy accorded the learning of skills and performance competencies, in contrast to pure theory. Still other forces for change appear to emanate from the faculties themselves, perhaps as a result of interaction with adult students and alumni as well as professional colleagues. It is fortunate that as needs for new educational methods have become evident, innovations in allied fields such as adult education and management development have been available for adaptation. The next stage, which appears to have already begun with the Public Administration Teaching Conferences, is for the field to pioneer in the development of its own methodological innovations. There is room for a great deal more learning about how to better prepare students to function in the complex public sector.

Acknowledgment

The authors are grateful to the Beistle Research Fund in the L. P. Cookingham Institute for support for this study and to Diana Hale, research fellow, for her assistance.

Notes

1. Sherwood, F. P. Innovations in Teaching Public Administration. *Proceedings of the Conference on Teaching Public Administration and Affairs.* Kansas City, Mo., 1978.
2. Buchanan, P. C. (ed.) *An Approach to Executive Development in Government: The Federal Executive Institute Experience.* National Academy of Public Administration, Washing, D.C., 1973.
3. Fletcher, T. W. (ed.) Symposium on Continuing Education for Public Administration. *Public Administration Review 33* (November/December 1976):487–532.

4. Fritschler, A. L. and Mackelprang, A. M. Graduate Education in Public Affairs/Public Administration: Results of the 1975 Survey. *Public Administration Review 37* (September/October 1977):488–494.
5. Waldo, D. Education for public administration in the seventies, in Mosher, F. C. (ed.), *American Public Administration: Past Present and Future,* University, Alabama, University of Alabama Press, Ala., 1975.
6. *Guidelines and Standards for Professional Master's Degree Programs in Public Affairs/Public Administration,* National Association of Schools of Public Affairs and Administration, Washington, D.C., 1974.
7. Knowles, M. S. *The Adult Education Movement in the U.S.* Robert E. Krieger Publishing Co., Huntington, N.Y., 1977.
8. Knowles, M. S. *The Adult Learner: A Neglected Species.* Gulf Publishing Co., Houston, 1973.
9. Knowles, op. cit.
10. Kolb, D. A., Rubin, I. M. and McIntyre, J. M. *Organizational Psychology: An Experiential Approach.* Prentice-Hall, Englewood Cliffs, N.J., 1974.
11. Hall, D. T., Bowen, D. B., Lewicki, R. J., and Hall, F. S. *Experiences in Management and Organizational Behavior.* St. Clair Press, Chicago, 1975.
12. The founding editor of *Exchange* is David L. Bradford. David's father is Leland P. Bradford, founder in the 1940s of the Adult Education Division of the National Education Association which developed "laboratory education" or sensitivity training, one of the earliest widely used experiential adult education techniques.
13. Fritschler and Mackelprang, op. cit.
14. Paige, D. Student perceptions of non-traditional public administration programs at U.S.F. *Proceedings of the Third National Conference on the Teaching of Public Administration.* Olympia, Washington, 1980.
15. Sherwood, op. cit.
16. Heise, J. A. Delivering a mid-career MPA program far from hearth and home. *Proceedings of the Third National Conference on the Teaching of Public Administration,* Olympia, Washington, 1980.
17. Figliola, C. L. Meeting the Needs of the In-Service Professional: Developing and Delivering Academic Programs for the 1980s. National Association of Schools of Public Administration and Affairs, National Conference. San Antonio, Tex., 1980.
18. A Plan for Improving Management Skills of Employees and Officials in the Virgin Islands Government." College of the Virgin Islands, unpublished manuscript, 1979.
19. Wessel, R. I. Continuing Education and Its Side Effects: An Answer to Cutback Management at Universities. Iowa State University, unpublished manuscript, 1980.

20. Weinberg, M. Off-Campus Public Administration Program at Ohio University. American Society for Public Administration Annual Conference, San Francisco, 1980.
21. Giallourakis, M. MPSA: a non-graditional graduate degree program for full time working professionals. *Proceedings of the Second National Conference on the Teaching of Public Administration*, Memphis, 1979.
22. Weinberg, op. cit.
23. Laudicina, E. Methods and measures of life experience assessment in public administration. *Proceedings of the National Conference on the Teaching of Public Administration and Affairs*. Kansas City, Mo., 1978.
24. Eddy, W. B. Designing experiential methods for non-behavioral courses. *Proceedings of the Third National Conference on the Teaching of Public Administration*. Olympia, Wash., 1980.
25. Brown, F. G. Three Types of Experiential Learning: A Non-Trivial Distinction. Conference on the Programmatic Use of Experiential Learning, Dallas, 1978.
26. Wolf, J. F. Experiential Learning in Professional Education: Concepts and Tools. *New Directions for Experiential Learning 8* (1980):17–26.
27. Chisholm, R. F. Experience-based learning for part-time MPA students. *Proceedings of the Second National Conference on Teaching Public Administration*. Memphis, 1979.
28. Harrison, R. and Hopkins, R. L. The Design of Cross-Cultural Training: An Alternative to the University Model. *Journal of Applied Behavioral Science 4* (1967):431–460.
29. Kolb, D. A. Learning and problem solving, in Kolb, D. A., Rubin, I. M., and McIntyre, J. M. (eds.) *Organizational Psychology*. Prentice Hall, Englewood Cliffs, N. J., 1974.
30. Evans, L., Hall, M., and Rinehart, J. Innovative Curriculum and Teaching Methods in Credit and Non-Credit Public Administration Courses for Adults: Some Problems and Some Suggestions. *National Conference on Public Administration*, Baltimore, 1979.
31. Klingner, D. E. Teaching the Realities of Public Personnel Management. *Public Personnel Management 40* (March–April 1979):95–100.
32. Eddy, op. cit.
33. Skruber, R. and Rizzo, A. Democracy in the Classroom: A Student Centered Approach to Evaluation. American Society for Public Administration National Conference, San Francisco, 1980.
34. Denhardt, R. B. On the Management of Public Service Education. *Southern Review of Public Administration 3* (December 1979):273–283.

35. Figliola, C. L. The Needs of In-Service Students: Are They Non-Traditional? American Society for Public Administration National Conference, San Francisco, 1980.

36. Wolf, J. F. Career assessment in graduate public administration education programs. *Proceedings of the National Conference on the Teaching of Public Administration.* Kansas City, Mo., 1978.

37. Mocker, D. W. and Spear, G. E. Needs assessment, in Langerman, P. D. and Smith, D. H. (eds) *Managing Adult and Continuing Education Program and Staff.* National Association for Public Continuing and Adult Education, Washington, D.C., 1979.

38. Denhardt, R. B. and Kirkhart, L. J. Administrative Education: An Alternative View. Unpublished manuscript, 1979.

39. Skruber and Rizzo, op. cit. (See chapter 7 in this volume.)

40. Denhardt, op. cit.

41. White, O. The Concept of Administrative Praxis. *Journal of Comparative Administration 4* (May 1973):55–86.

42. Jreisat, J. Public Administration and the Theory/Practice Controversy. *Southern Review of Public Administration 1* (March 1978):503–509.

43. Eddy, W. B. Interpersonal skill training in public administration education. *Proceedings of the National Conference on the Teaching of Public Administration and Affairs,* Kansas City, Mo., 1978.

44. Zauderer, D. G. and Ross, B. H. Curriculum Reform and Organizational Culture: Public Administration at the American University. *Urban Analysis 3* (1976):187–196.

45. Greenhill, M., Metz, C, and Stander, P. Formulation and Assessment of Public Administration Educational Objectives to Optimize Learning in Adults and Other "Non-Traditional" Students. Unpublished manuscript. City University of New York, 1978.

7

Democracy in the Classroom:
a student-centered approach to evaluation

Richard Skruber and Ann-Marie Rizzo
Florida International University, North Miami, Florida

It is one thing to discuss the whys and wherefores of democracy and education; it is quite another matter to attempt to practice democracy's principles in the classroom. Many efforts to provide a democratic framework in both design and operation have relied mainly on course content and other structural variables—the nature of the discipline, type of program, student make-up, and so forth. Regardless of the degree of educational democracy present, one area not explored in great depth is that of student evaluation. Even if taught according to andragogical principles (i.e., the teaching and learning of adults as distinguished from the education of children), students in most courses are evaluated by pedagogical methods. The great contradiction in teaching adults as if they were children has been reported elsewhere,[1] andragogical approaches to evaluation on the other hand, have seldom been discussed.

This chapter will attempt to remedy this deficiency by examining pedagogical and andragogical models of evaluation, a method of evaluating professional skills based on adult education principles, and an example of this method used in the classroom.

The Pedagogical Model and Evaluation

Pedagogy is usually defined as the art and science of teaching children. Several value assumptions accompanying this definition are worth mentioning. One assumption is that those who learn are dependent upon the teacher for guidance, direction, and evaluation of their learning. In fact, the teacher is the sole authority for the student's education. She or he structures the learning environment with the subject matter in mind. Course objectives emanate from the subject matter, nor from the students' learning needs. In this sense, the subject matter and course objectives are inviolate. They assume an objective status in which their value assumptions are beyond question.

This notion of subject-centered education is reinforced by a view of the student as *tabula rasa* or blank slate. The teacher "spoon feeds" knowledge while the student digests and regurgitates it appropriately. Again, little flexibility is allowed for those who perform poorly under these constraints. According to this model, the students who perform best have learned that their role is a passive one. They are dependent upon the teacher for their grade, and if they follow the teacher's rules, the appropriate grade will be awarded. The end product of this process is that students earning enough of the right kind of grades receive their diplomas.

At this juncture, we can isolate three components of the pedagogical model that apply to evaluation. Student evaluation can be defined as:

A grade: Rather than evaluate the individual's learning through a comprehensive, written assessment which focuses on developmental activities, letter grades or credit-no credit formats are employed.

For student performance: The teacher assigns the learning objectives, assigns the tasks, determines the method and criteria of evaluation and the student performs within these parameters. The emphasis here is on performance as the output or measure of learning, not learning itself, which is, of course, a cognitive, intrapsychic process.

Carried out by the teacher: The teacher is the source of evaluation. The student does not usually participate in assessment in a meaningful manner although some attempts at self-assessment and peer evaluation occasionally occur.

A Critique of the Pedagogical Model

As the reader has probably already inferred, there are several flawed assumptions with the pedagogical model: (1) the teacher serves as sole authority in the evaluation process; (2) the students are not capable of directing and evaluating their own learning; and (3) the subject matter is the primary, even sole determinant of how the course is taught and how students must learn. Taking each defect in turn, we will explore them in greater detail.

We address the first issue by tracing how teachers learn the authoritative role. Generally, educational institutions begin to confer authority upon teachers through their early professional socialization. As they progress further up the elaborate ladder of credentialling and degree garnering, they learn to place importance on teacher authority. They will, after all, receive their "union cards," as some cynically label them, by obeying the rules of the academic game. Once in an academic position, official job descriptions and institutional sanctions augmented by informal role negotiations will further support the notion that the teacher is the sole authority in the classroom. After all those years of surviving the rigors of traditional, pedagogical instructional methods themselves, the neophyte teacher's first natural response is to exercise his or her power over students, perhaps by observing gleefully, "It's my turn!" The resultant "junior professor syndrome" is rather widespread for these reasons.

Nevertheless, over the course of teaching the instructor may eventually discover that greater exercise of authority over students seems directly related to passive, obedient behavior. Students are too seldom motivated to learn for the pure joy of it. Knowles for example believes that adults learn more readily when internally motivated than externally rewarded or sanctioned by the carrot or stick of grades.[2] Verduin et al. support this notion:

> The motivation to learn something is present if the individual can see the personal meaning involved. If the goals for instruction are not those of the learner, the content will have little or no meaning for him. Unless he can see the personal meaning involved, it is doubtful if real learning (behavioral change) will occur in the adult student.[3]

The relationship between teacher authority and a student's direction over his or her learning is depicted in Figure 1.

The Teacher-Student Relationship Continuum reveals that teacher authority and student autonomy are inversely related. On the left hand side of the continuum, the pedagogical model is demonstrated by the teacher retaining sole authority over evaluation and the student characteristically making little or no input. On the right hand side is the andragogical model where teacher authority is infrequently exercised for its own sake and students learn in a self-directed and responsible manner. In short, they enjoy autonomy over their learning.

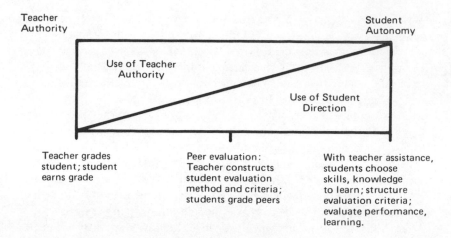

Teacher
Authority

Student
Autonomy

Use of Teacher
Authority

Use of Student
Direction

| Teacher grades student; student earns grade | Peer evaluation: Teacher constructs student evaluation method and criteria; students grade peers | With teacher assistance, students choose skills, knowledge to learn; structure evaluation criteria; evaluate performance, learning. |

Figure 1 A continuum of teacher-student relationship in evaluation.

This formulation also addresses the second flawed assumption of the pedagogical model. According to Verduin, Knowles, and others, adults are not only capable of self-direction and self-assessment, they enjoy participating in decisions regarding their own learning. The extent of involvement is therefore directly related to the quantity and quality of their learning.

Finally, the subject-centered approach where course content dictates how a course should be taught and evaluated must be questioned. In the classroom, it is often the case that the field of knowledge is preeminent, that is, course content is more important than how or to what degree a student learns. If students question the relevance of the topic or find that a particular instructional method does not help them learn, it is their responsibility to seek an alternative. A student who has difficulty learning specific material may be encouraged to obtain remedial coursework or tutorial assistance. The student is found at fault since the material cannot be altered to suit one individual's learning deficiencies. Once again, the course material and ensuing objectives form the mold into which the student must fit.

In addressing this perspective several points can be made. Course content will retain its integrity no matter how it is taught. A course in quantitative techniques is not limited to rote memorization and homework; real life applications can greatly enhance the relevance of the subject for the student, making statistical techniques more useful and meaningful in the process.[4] Such a course might not match the potential of a group dynamics course with its great variety of teaching and learning techniques and experiential methods.

Nevertheless, course content need not dictate orthodoxy in course presentation or limit experimentation, nor should the course be considered "soft" or easy simply because nontraditional teaching methods are used.

Teachers' expertise should also remain intact. If their expertise were limited to presenting course material by the lecture method alone, we would severely underestimate their ability to transmit information, stimulate and challenge students, and help them learn. It is to be hoped that teachers possess a firmer base of legitimacy in scholarship and the academic enterprise than such a misjudgment of their abilities would imply.

To further encourage the adoption of adult education techniques we should add that universities and colleges generally allow substantial academic freedom to instructors for course design and implementation. In many cases, experimentation with nontraditional methods is not only tolerated but encouraged. In this light, we believe that more democratic notions of teacher-student learning relationships can be attempted when pedagogical techniques prove inadequate. Students, especially adult students, should be meaningfully involved in their own intellectual development, not simply as passive recipients of education (in the manner of one who attends class, earns a grade, receives a certificate, and therefore can be said to be educated) but as active participants in learning.

The Andragogical Model and Evaluation

The andragogical approach to education can be summarized as follows. First, adults can learn. While aging may slow down the learning process, this reduction in capacities is so minimal and occurs so gradually that it cannot disrupt the inherent learning capabilities of adults.

Second, real learning is an internal process. Contrary to the "garbage in - garbage out" model, adult educators view learning as highly personal, controlled by the learner, and engaging the whole being. When genuine learning occurs, it is accompanied by observable changes in behavior. True learning cannot be measured or evaluated in precisely the same manner as mere absorption of information.

Finally, the special climate and conditions of learning and the teacher's facilitative role illustrate the principles of adult education. Although the many aspects of these conditions cannot be covered here, a few can be mentioned.

Table 1 incorporates a radically different view of human nature than witnessed in the pedagogical model. Theory Y-type assumptions apply not only

Table 1 A Summary of Conditions and Behaviors Essential
for Adult Learning

Conditions of Learning	The Teacher's Role
Learners:	Teacher helps learners:
feel a need to learn	diagnose the gap between goals and performance
identify goals of learning as their own	
	build relationships of mutual trust and support for learning
feel responsible for planning and carrying out the learning experience	
	set learning objectives in which needs of students, the institution, the teacher, the subject matter and society are taken into account
participate actively in learning	
have a sense of progress toward their goals	

Source: Adapted from Knowles, M. *The Modern Practice of Adult Education*, Association Press, New York, 1977. (See Ref. 1).

to student behavior but the teacher's as well. In place of exercising authority
for its own sake, the teacher intervenes with controlling behavior—directing,
leading, organizing—only when additional structure is required by the student.
In terms of furthering cognitive development, students may also require sum-
marizing, critiquing, analyzing, and questioning behavior. In any case, the
teacher serves as a resource person and diagnostician, creating a climate conducive to learning, providing information sources, and intervening in a student's activity when his learning plan goes awry. The ultimate goal is to
augment the student's independence or autonomy in achieving academic
goals. Thus, the student is engaging in metaeducation—learning how to learn.

In this light, the core of andragogy is found in the ability of learners to
evaluate themselves. Andragogy

> prescribes a process of self-evaluation in which the teacher devotes his
> energy to helping adults get evidence for themselves about the progress
> they are making towards their educational goals. In this process, the
> strengths and weaknesses of the educational program itself must be
> assessed in terms of how it has facilitated or inhibited the learning of
> the students. So evaluation is a mutual undertaking.[5]

This self-diagnostic attitude also extends to student performance of specific behaviors. Here, we are interested in helping the learner objectively assess the current level of performance of a selected sample of behaviors important at a given time in his or her development. The objective is to decide where and how to invest time and energy in improving performance to reach a desired skill level, rather than to rehearse behaviors until that performance level is reached.

Ultimately, participants in this process will gain a perspective on their strengths and weaknesses in respect to their original model of desired performance. In the process, they will find that their aspirations concerning desirable performance levels have risen. Upon discovering this, new goals are set and the cycle begins anew.[6]

In sum, andragogy means that students possess the ability to diagnose learning needs, to develop plans to achieve specified goals, and to evaluate their progress or performance. Learning how to learn in the fullest sense means learning how to internalize the evaluation process to serve one's personal needs. Here, evaluation is an internal, highly personal process quite different from the external, institutionalized process typical of pedagogical approaches. Without a genuine self-assessment capability, adult education approaches lack the power to transform the student into a self-directed, motivated, and autonomous life-long learner. If this type of learner is our goal, then adult educators must begin to experiment with workable and meaningful student-directed evaluation techniques.

The Student Certification Process

We have been exploring the possibilities of a learner-directed approach that can be adapted to a variety of coursework. This model is based on the transfer of expertise from teacher to student through "authorizing" students to certify each other in acquiring behavioral skills. This student certification (SC) process features:

1. Student participation in the determination of behavioral skills appropriate to specified tasks within a particular course context;
2. Students setting evaluation standards and criteria for the assessment of performance;
3. Students becoming "certified" in a particular skill according to their own specified criteria;
4. Students certifying other students in performing the skill.

The process fundamentally operates along these lines. The course is organized around a set of skills to be learned in conjunction with the course content. While this suggests that this process is applicable primarily to experiential or competency-based course formats, conceptual or higher-order cognitive skills may be integrated with behavioral skills for more innovative learning experiences with some imaginative course design on the part of teachers. The skills to be learned may be determined by the teacher or may be decided jointly by the teacher and students, as is the case in the example outlined in this chapter.

Once the skills have been determined, the students are organized into teams which are responsible for conducting one or more certification sessions. Under the guidance of the teacher, the teams are responsible for researching literature pertinent to the skill, operationalizing the skill into specific criteria of performance, designing a certification activity, and conducting a certification class session. When this work is complete, the teacher uses the process designed by the certification team to certify the team members themselves. In this way, team members become expert in the skill. After certification, the team is then authorized to certify others in the skill.

Using this process, students are involved in setting the goals, standards, and evaluation criteria and in authoritative assessment of their own performance. The skills themselves vary, depending upon the nature of the course and course objectives. The SC approach can be easily adapted to a variety of organizational behavior, group dynamics, principles of management and organizational development, or change courses. We have used it primarily in our courses Administrator and the Legislative Process[7] and Public Personnel Administration. It is the latter course we will describe in some detail.

Student Certification in a Public Personnel Course

The Public Personnel Administration course is required to complete the master's degree program. Its goals are:

1. To describe the special nature of personnel administration in the public sector;
2. To address the relationship between personnel and other sub-systems in public organizations;
3. To survey a range of approaches and techniques to improve existing personnel practices;
4. To present the functions critical to effective personnel management; and

5. To develop expertise in certain selected behaviors necessary to carry out these personnel functions.

It is the fifth goal which will form the backdrop for our experiment in student certification. In the class, to gain a perspective on training, we have students performing the training function or role of a personnel administrator. The class members decide their training interests by individually listing in order of preference which behavioral skills important to a personnel administrator they would like to acquire. Then Delphi-fashion, these results are tabulated, interpreted, consolidated, and fed back until agreement is reached by individuals in four or five areas (depending on class size). For example, in one class, the first ranking resulted in 8 to 10 topics with a variety of definitions in each topic area as to, for example, what interviewing meant: Did it include performance appraisal interviews, only employment interviews or both? By the third ranking, all students had narrowed their preferences to one of four topics; values clarification as a technique for career development, employment (hiring) interviews, communications, and performance appraisal. Groups were then organized around topics, not vice-versa. This has both advantages and disadvantages. The advantages are primarily in terms of serving individual interests; the disadvantage is that groups may include incompatible members or some who do not perform well in groups, shirk responsibilities, and so forth. In any case, all the normal dynamics of group interaction are present that should be discussed and resolved by the end of the course.

Once the topics are decided, students must follow certain steps in the design and execution of the training. Using the example of hiring interviews, the process can be summarized as follows.

1. Design a training program in the form of one self-contained training activity;
2. Design training objectives and formulate evaluation criteria to be used in certification of trainees;
3. Carry out the activity and become certified by the instructor(s);
4. Train other students in interviewing skills by the following steps:
   a. Present the background to interviewing—concepts, approaches, procedures, "do's and don'ts"—and provide the final certification form for trainees.
   b. Present the activity, for example, an interviewing role play with prepared, well-defined roles for interviewer and interviewee. This presentation by trainers will represent the role model, demonstrating pertinent behavioral skills with appropriate standards. The role modelling will conclude with trainers relating the certification

form to the role model, indicating failure or success in meeting the criteria in specific, operational, and measurable terms.

c. Student trainees will rehearse the behavior with another role play situation provided by trainers. It will also include well-defined role descriptions.

d. After the role play, trainers will "coach" trainees, providing constructive feedback using the certification form as the major impetus.

e. Trainers and trainees discuss the performance.

f. The process is repeated with usually a different role play or exercise.

g. "Coaching" and discussion (steps *d* and *e*) are repeated until trainees exhibit behavior in accordance with principles presented in step *a* and operationalized during "coaching" or until the time limit is reached.

Step *a* requires the most preparation since research material must be identified and organized for the class presentation and, very important, the certification form must be designed. This usually demands several rounds of subsubmission, reaction by the instructor, and revision to incorporate suggestions. About a third of the way through the course and well before actual training is to take place, each group presents its certification form to the class for its reaction. This step is taken since: (1) the trainees should be able to respond to the trainers' goals and standards; and (2) it is a learning process for the class as well. Often, the class observes that the forms are incomplete, unrealistic or, very commonly, contain unmeasurable or insignificant criteria. For example, one group held that the criterion of "not shaking one's feet" while sitting during an interview deserved inclusion, whereas the class overwhelmingly disagreed. (It was later struck from the form.)

During the training activity itself, the group must present the final certification form, this time for implementation purposes and not subject to class approval. This is done to consolidate the trainees' understanding of both the evaluation criteria and standards for performance. During the role model itself, standards and criteria are indicated as well as during steps *d* and *e*. Therefore, certification principles are employed during the entire training sequence. In this manner, evaluation criteria and standards are defined, applied and tested, defended or, in the early stages (step 2), modified.

A great deal of preparation is involved in this sequence of events, since most students are not at first able to articulate standards for performance of a behavioral skill or specify criteria in measurable, operational terms. To be able to do so requires a great deal of coaching from the instructor and much tolerance for ambiguity from students as well. Students frequently exhibit a high level of anxiety regarding the entire process and some counterdependency characteristically follows: "You're the teacher [the expert], *you* tell us the answer" is a not uncommon refrain. The strategy here is to press the students to provide the answers—any other response would not encourage formulation of their own ideas.

The inability to conceive criteria in concrete, specific, measurable terms is frequently encountered. Some students believe, for example, that a positive climate is important in effective interviewing but resist breaking this global concept into specific behavioral components. Others argue that smiling or eye contact is important. If we inquire how the evaluation categories *superior, average, fair,* or *poor* will be applied to *smiling* or *eye contact,* a great deal of consternation inevitably results. Our basic stance is if it is indeed a critical behavior, it can be specified, standardized, observed, and measured.

Some Final Notes

In summing up the pluses for the use of student certification several outcomes come foremost to mind: learning appears to be more concrete and lasting, and the students (as well as the instructor) have fun and enjoy learning. Although the former is of more importance to most educators, the latter is most impressive since it implies that the motivation to learn is related to the extent of student involvement in designing the learning experience.

In addition, when authority over classroom activities is shared by the instructor, students feel an increased sense of responsibility for their own learning. Having a great deal more vested interest in learning, students behave more as "citizens" rather than as wards of the class. This democratic environment seems to promote a healthy attitude toward learning, especially when students are asked to share authority in the evaluation process.

This is of course not a definitive solution to the problem of evaluation, and there are some problems to be dealt with in the transfer of authority through the SC method. Some of these are the amount of time and energy required for individual and group consultation; the (for some) radical change in the instructor's role from one of traditional control over the classroom to one of coach, facilitator, and consultant; the anxiety encountered by the instructor in relinquishing authority in grading as well as student anxiety incurred by the SC process; and finally, the adaptability 6f courses to experiential or competency-based formats. Nevertheless, these problems can be resolved or at least minimized if college and university faculty adhere to and are supported in their goal of developing the individual through self-directed learning.

Acknowledgment

The authors would like to express their gratitude to Orion White for originating the concept of student certification.[8]

Notes

1. Knowles, M. *The Modern Practice of Adult Education.* Association Press, New York, 1977.
2. Ibid.
3. Verduin, J. R., Miller, H. G., and Greer, C. E. *Adults Teaching Adults.* Learning Concepts, Austin, 1977.
4. Thomas, J. E. lim $PA_{(QM)}$ = instructor understanding: student → graduation, in Rizzo, A. and Heimovics, R. (eds.) *Innovations in Teaching Public Affairs and Administration.* Kansas City: University of Missouri/ Florida International University, 1981, pp. 184–192.
5. Knowles, p. 43.
6. Ibid., pp. 280–297.
7. Rizzo, A. and Skruber, R. Wheeling and Dealing: A Simulation in Legislative-Administrative Behavior. *Exchange: The Organization Behavior Teaching Journal. 1* (Winter, 1980), pp. 31–34.
8. McSwain, C. J. and White, O. F. The Issue of Authority and the Learning Process: Founding Theory in Myths. *Southern Review of Public Administration. 3*(3) (December 1979).

8
Prolegomenon to a Teachable Theory of Public Administration

Guy B. Adams
Evergreen State College, Olympia, Washington

Theories presently in use in public administration classrooms are effectively unteachable, because they are essentially both abstract and irrelevant. This is true both from the standpoint of pedagogy and from the standpoint of the substance. Dwight Waldo, in his recent book, *The Enterprise of Public Administration*,[1] lists fourteen problem areas that face public administration as this century draws to a close: (1) decreasing growth and increasing scarcity, (2) economy, effectiveness, and efficiency under new and difficult circumstances, (3) trade-offs between hard and soft values, (4) proper amount and mix of professionalism and expertise, (5) unionism in the public sector, (6) values and mechanisms of centralization and decentralization, (7) racial-ethnic and sexual equality, (8) obsolescence of knowledge in public administration, (9) policymaking in and by the bureaucracy, (10) needs of the present and proximate future as against the needs of a more distant future, (11) staffing, managing and controlling new forms of organization, (12) developing less authoritarian, less bureaucratic organizations without at the same time permitting undesirable confusion, (13) increasing ethical complexity (and confusion), and (14) conflict and crises. This is a formidable list. The theories extant in public administration offer little hope of adequately informing the practice necessary to address it. Public administration theory is saddled with a grab-bag of theories begged, borrowed, or stolen from the social science disciplines. These theories address the problems of public administration listed above haphazardly at best. An adequate theory of public administration, one that is teachable, must address directly the problem sets which confront the public administrator in her or his concrete lived world. I intend to offer some tentative suggestions as to how such a theory of public administration might be developed.

The argument proceeds as follows. First, I discuss the present (lamentable) condition of theory in public administration. There are both epistemological and ideological difficulties with the theories presently in use. The epistemological difficulties stem largely from the conception of theory currently operative in the social sciences, from which public administration has borrowed. The ideological difficulties, following in part from the narrow construction of the theoretical enterprise in social science, stem largely from functional rationality and from liberalism, twin tenets of the Reform Era, which remain as rigid encrustations on our present understanding of the role and scope of public administration. Next, I argue that a teachable theory must integrate for the learner the process of learning with the content to be learned. Suggesting that epistemology is best seen as a process and that content is unavoidably ideological, I argue that a coherent integration of epistemological and ideological foundations is necessary for the development of a teachable theory of public administration. Finally, I propose some tentative ideas about what those foundations might look like.

The Present State of Theories in Public Administration

Within public administration education, as in social science education in general, theory and practice are dichotomized. The normative aim of building theory is prediction and control; practice becomes the technique of engineering that instrumental aim. In applied fields, like public administration, students are correctly concerned with practice. Except insofar as theory informs the various techniques of practice, why should students of public administration evidence concern for theories? Indeed, since most techniques in public administration are ill-informed theoretically,[2] the student need have no concern with theory at all.

Within academic programs there are almost no courses in public administration theory per se.[3] I think this is because academics in public administration themselves recognize the irrelevance of theories in public administration, and avoid teaching them. Of course, much theory is taught in public administration curricula, but it is parcelled out into discrete courses, for instance, organization theory, or theories of public finance, and so forth. Even in these cases, however, the most theoretical courses are often perceived by students as the least relevant to practice. Of course, this makes perfectly logical sense, given the existence of a theory-practice dichotomy.

The substantive content of theories in public administration is also inherently abstract and irrelevant, again because of its divorce from practice. Indeed, most of these theories have been borrowed from other disciplines, which are largely unconcerned, in any direct way, with practical applications. Denhardt and Denhardt observe:

> As an academic discipline, public administration has failed to produce a coherent and reflectively informed body of knowledge capable of connecting theory and practice and has instead become primarily interested in developing techniques to be used in efficiently pursuing established (though often outdated) purposes.[4]

It is no wonder that theories in public administration are so little taught, and then avoided when they are. Indeed, they are effectively unteachable.

Theory and Practice: The Epistemological Dimension

The problem of public administration theory, resulting in part from the theory-practice dichotomy, has both an epistemological dimension and an ideological dimension. The epistemological dimension of the problem arises from the conception of the nature of the theoretical enterprise held by mainstream social science. The theory-practice dichotomy goes hand in hand with a distinction between empirical theory (which explains and describes what is) and normative theory (which discusses what ought to be), and a distinction between fact and value. These are all features which have been identified with "positivist social science," which refers to,

> that metatheory of social science which is based on a modern empiricist philosophy of science often referred to as the hypethetico-deductive model of science. Its principle contemporary exponents are Carl Hempel, Karl Popper, and Ernst Nagel . . . there are four essential features of this

metatheory: first, drawing on the distinction between discovery and valid-
ation, its deductive-nomological account of explanation and concomitant
modified Humean interpretation of the notion of cause; second, its belief
in a neutral observation language as the proper foundation of knowledge;
third, its value-free ideal of scientific knowledge; and fourth, its belief in
the methodological unity of the sciences.[5]

The conception of theory intrinsic to "positivist social science" has been
termed "systematic theory."[6] The aim of systematic theory is to develop a
set of interconnected generalizations (or, in some formulations, causal laws)
which explain phenomena in a given area of inquiry and which are derived
from or established by empirically-tested hypotheses. Richard Bernstein in
The Restructuring of Social and Political Theory shows by means of an extended discussion of the work of Robert Merton and Neil Smelser, two highly
respected social scientists, the extent to which this view of the social scientific
enterprise is pervasive.[7] What is so deeply curious is that after some 30 years
of empirical research by legions of social scientists, we have virtually no systematic theory anywhere in the social sciences:

> there is an extensive and growing body of literature that reveals the empir-
> ical, methodological, logical and ideological inadequacies of empirical theo-
> ries, including "functional theories," "equilibrium theories," "systems the-
> ories," and "social exchange theories." While there are vehement disputes
> about how fruitful these theories really are, and in what sense, if any, they
> approximate the ideal of empirical theory, no responsible social scientist has
> asserted that we have yet achieved anything comparable to what was achieved
> in sixteenth and seventeenth-century physical science.[8]

And it must be remembered that the achievements of sixteenth- and seventeenth-century physical science were accomplished by a relative handful of
scientists, by comparison with the vast cohorts of social scientists toiling in
the empirical vineyards these last 30 years.

Moreover, there seems to be a growing divergence between the "common
sense" actions of persons and the accounts of those actions offered by social
scientists. This is especially critical for theory to bear any relevance for an
applied field. An important reason for this divergence is the loss of the world
of everyday life:

> More and more, social science retreats from any attempt to comprehend
> man in the actual context of his immediate experience, his life-world. An
> element of the absurd enters the scene of the sociologist's performance:

once the teleological bond between action and justification is severed, the activity of the investigator is reduced to conceptual rubble.[9]

Clearly, a different conception of theory is required in order to suggest an epistemologically adequate and teachable public administration theory.

Theory in public administration (and elsewhere in the social realm) should not pretend to provide solutions to problems (as in mathematics) or to discover laws (as in physical science). Rather it should strive to provide both the inquirer and practitioner with a conceptual framework useful in making sense of the situation which they confront.:

> Theoretical formulations hover so low over the interpretations they govern that they don't make much sense or hold much interest apart from them. This is so not because they are not general (if they are not general, they are not theoretical), but because, stated independently of their applications, they seem either commonplace or vague.[10]

The theories presently in use in public administration are far removed from their applications (in the various disciplines),[11] and suffer mightily from being vague or otherwise irrelevant.

Theory and Practice: The Ideological Dimension

There is also an ideological dimension to the problem of public administration theory. Most theories in public administration are predicated on functional rationality and liberalism. Functional rationality (the rationalized ordering of acts within a means-ends sequence) is a truncated and historically deformed conception of rationality.[12] For the bulk of recorded history, functional rationality was never more than an aspect of the broader concept of rationality, until the rise of market society and its concomitant economic reasoning. Rationality, within the history of human thought, had always been more broadly construed, incorporating both ethical and normative, as well as merely instrumental, aspects.[13] In modern times, however, when we speak of the continuing rationalization of society, we mean functional rationalization.

Liberalism, inspired by the seventeenth-century writing of John Locke, can be reasonably described as the political theory of the market economy. It is no accident that liberalism has become so closely tied to economics, with its emphasis on contracts and property rights.[14] The present view of liberalism emphasizes three chief features:[15] (1) Political democracy is seen as a mechanism for choosing governments, (2) man is defined as a maximizing consumer and appropriator, and (3) society is conceived as a network of market relations. Politics is thus reduced to economics:

> The particular harm that a century of liberalism has accomplished—to be
> sure, along with some progressive achievements—has been to trap much of
> the human spirit of emancipation within the false imagery of individualistic
> pursuit of happiness and civil liberties. Liberals have persistently tended to
> cut the citizen off from the person; and they have placed on their human-
> istic pedestal a cripple of a man, a man without a moral or political nature;
> a man with plenty of contractual rights and obligations, perhaps, but a man
> without moorings in any real community. . . . [16]

The combination of liberalism and functional rationality has been a particularly powerful one in this country during this century. Indeed, an examination of
a typology of theories of public administration serves to illustrate that functional rationality and liberalism underpin every major conception of the field
of public administration.

   The typology, developed by George Frederickson, lists six major models of
public administration, which include (1) classic bureaucratic, (2) neobureaucratic, (3) institutional, (4) human relations, (5) public choice, and (6)
new public administration.[17] The *classic bureaucratic* model, seen as descriptive of much public administration today, is concerned with both the structure
of the bureaucracy and the way both people and work are managed and controlled in the organization. The latter follows the thinking of Max Weber,
whereas the former stems in part from the writing of Frederick W. Taylor.
The *neobureaucratic* model focuses on decision making as the unit of analysis,
while the means of analysis are quantitative. Management science and operations research are representative of this model. The *institutional* model arose
from the behavioral movement in the social sciences and seeks to provide descriptive or explanatory theories of organizations. Pluralism and incremental-
ism are dominant features of these theories. The *human relations* model focuses on the growth and development of the worker in the organization. It
posits that the satisfied worker is more productive for the organization. The
public choice model applies nonmarket economics to public administration.
By decentralizing services, governmental jurisdictions essentially compete in
offering services to the citizen, who chooses a government in much the same
way he or she chooses a product. The *new public administration* seeks to ren-
der public organizations more democratic, decentralized, and humanistic, and
aims at having services provided more equitably to members of society.

   None of these models provides a way for the public administrator to construe his or her tasks more broadly. The concern for efficiency, the focus on
the internal functioning of the bureau is always in the forefront. These models

are largely indifferent to the *context* within which administrative action occurs. Administrative behavior can be functionally rationalized as easily in the Third Reich as in a social welfare agency. When there is some concern with context, as most notably in new public administration and in public choice, it is still safely within the confines of liberalism—individual rights are broadened and "equal opportunity" enhanced. The grip of liberalism and functional rationalization on all of these models of public administration is firm.

The thrust of Frederickson's argument, however, is more than the presentation of the typology; rather it is to suggest that the new public administration traces its lineage in a very direct way to various of the earlier models. The new public administration, therefore, is not particularly new. Indeed, the entire field of public administration, including the new public administration, has always been characterized by the assumptions of the Reform Era—that is, liberalism and functional rationalization. The field had its origin in the Reform Era in American history, and has never deviated substantially from the parameters set out at that time. In the intervening years, the underlying epistemological and ideological framework has become even more rigidified.

As James Weinstein has shown so persuasively in *The Corporate Ideal in the Liberal State: 1900-1918*, the Reform Era saw the striking of a bargain between business, government, and labor which has remained substantially unaltered since that time.[18] The bargain commits each partner essentially to grease the skids of the free enterprise system, and especially the corporate interests therein. This bargain committed government in the United States to be little more than a handmaiden to free enterprise. The subsequent New Deal and trappings of the welfare state were tolerable under the terms of the bargain until their growth threatened the untrammeled operation of free enterprise. The pervasiveness of the bargain has been manifest in the countless state and local political campaigns that have been fought and won even during the heyday of the welfare state under the rubric of "bringing business methods into government." Ronald Reagan's recent election merely confirms the continuing strength of the bargain that was struck nearly three quarters of a century ago.

I would argue that no theory of *public* administration can be ideologically adequate until we, in this country, begin to construe government as a positive agent for social, political, and economic interests. It is axiomatic that even a "nonpolicy" of total economic deregulation creates a pattern of social and economic distribution that one can interpret as more or less just or unjust. All debates and decisions about the relative justice of distributions are fundamentally *public* acts. Not debating the issue at all is a *public* act, albeit a distorted and degenerate one. Not deciding by letting the status quo determine the distribution is a *public* act, although equally distorted and degenerate. We must renew this debate and learn to entrust government as a positive agent to implement our decisions, our public will. Of course, this position represents socialism. While the rubric is not widely tolerated, the public debate over just distribution is very much a part of the American tradition.[19] It is this part of our tradition that must find nurture if we are to have an ideologically adequate theory of public administration, indeed, if in the end we are to have any *public* administration at all. The Faustian bargain of the Reform Era carried to its extreme eliminates *public* administration altogether. The Reaganite movement's national discrediting of the public service is illustrative of this tendency.

In summary, the ideology of the Reform Era, resting on functional rationality and on liberalism, is fundamentally flawed and patently inadequate in meeting the agenda of problems set forth by Waldo and listed at the beginning of this chapter. A stronger ideological foundation, one that is compatible with epistemological requirements and that is learner-centered, one that fosters a *public* administration, seems called for.

Toward a Teachable Theory of Public Administration

A teachable theory of public administration can be developed through the utilization of more nearly adequate epistemological and ideological foundations. Much as the problem of public administration theory may be seen as rooted in the inadequacies of mainstream social science, a more satisfactory view of social science—interpretive social science—may be used to found a teachable public administration theory. Interpretive social science suggests that social behavior can only be accounted for by using "action concepts."[20] Action concepts describe doings rather than happenings (e.g., jumping is something someone does, whereas falling happens to someone). "Action concepts are employed to describe behavior which is done with a purpose such that one can ask, what is its point, aim or intent, or what was the person trying to do, desiring or meaning."[21] The use of action concepts takes one, of necessity, past the mere observation of behavior; it requires an *interpretation* on the part of the observer. The process of inquiry becomes a communicative act. Thus, the effect of an interpretive social science is to foster dialogue in speaking and acting between individuals or even within oneself.

> ... by revealing what it is that people are doing, i.e., by revealing the rules and assumptions upon which they are acting, it makes it possible for us to engage in a dialogue with them—we understand, as it were, the language of their social life.[22]

The epistemological aim of interpretive social science—that is, the understanding of social action—is complemented by an ideological aim—the fostering of undistorted communication, which is requisite for democracy. The ideological aim is further informed by the pedagogical goal of enlightening and thus empowering social actors so that, as they become conscious of the structural conditions impinging on themselves and others, they can make choices about their posture toward those conditions.[23]

Interpretive social science, then, represents a framework within which a teachable theory of public administration can be developed. The pedagogical requirement for a teachable theory is that it be centered on the learner: " . . . rather than emphasizing content, as does the traditional method, or the teaching relationship and learning 'community' of the process orientation, what we do is *ground* our educational method by focusing on how both content and process bear on the learner's total development as a person."[24] Thus, a teachable theory requires an integration of process and content aimed at the growth of the person, just as a substantively adequate theory requires an integration of epistemology and ideology aimed at the growth of human culture. That the substantive requirements for a theory of public administration parallel the requirements for a teachable theory is not merely fortuitous. It follows from a recognition that epistemology is fundamentally a (communicative) process and that content is irretrievably ideological.

Epistemological Foundations

The epistemological roots of interpretive social science and therefore of a teachable theory of public administration are in phenomenology and its concept of the life-world. Phenomenology and its outgrowth, existentialism, have been the major development in European philosophy in this century. Perhaps the basic appeal of phenomenology is that it overcomes the problems associated with the objectivist methodology inherent in contemporary social science. Moreover, it does so without lapsing into an equally untenable subjectivism. The key dilemma of objectivist epistemology seems to be reconciling the intrinsic conflict between man, as an *active* observer, studying man, as a *passive* object. This dilemma creates a fundamental subject-object dichotomy—man is irrevocably alienated from what he studies.

Phenomenology seeks to resolve this dilemma primarily by moving beyond the usual formulation of the problem. It accomplishes this by offering a "third way" which cannot be fairly characterized as either objectivist or subjectivist. This third way was inspired by the philosophy of Edmund Husserl, the founder of modern phenomenology.[25] The key assertion of Husserlian phenomenology is that the foundation of knowing rests in human consciousness. The "essence" of any "object" of investigation is to be found in the consciousness of the knowing subject. A corollary to this assertion is the "intentionality" of consciousness, that is, consciousness is always consciousness *of something*. These insights enabled Husserl, in analyzing human consciousness, to distinguish between the *noesis*, or thought (related to, or directed at, objects), and the *noema*, or object (in thought). Knowledge arises out of the interplay between "subject" (*noesis*) and "object" (*noema*) occurring in the context of human consciousness. Knowledge, then, is fundamentally relational.

Later thinkers in the phenomenological tradition focussed on hermeneutics, the art of interpretation (which inspired the model of interpretive social science mentioned earlier)[26] Interpretation is directed at understanding (as contrasted with, but not excluding, explanation or description), and affords the opportunity to grasp the fundamental historicity of the life-world and its layered and textured experience.

The life-world is a concept which seeks to return thought or reflection to the only "real" world, the world of everyday life, the world which we all share. Husserl has suggested the vividness of the life-world as follows:

> To live is always to live-in-certainty-of-the world. Waking life is being a-wake to the world, being constantly and directly "conscious" of the world and of oneself as living *in* the world, actually experiencing and actually effecting the ontic certainty of the world.[27]

On a more personal, or existential, level, Maurice Natanson portrays the life-world as follows:

> Expressed in first person terms, I am thrust into a world which is always "already" in process, that is, for me, the actor on the social scene, the participant in daily life, there is no point at which it could be said that the slate is clean, experience is untouched by the past, or everything is just starting.[28]

The life-world, then, is the world as we encounter it in direct and immediate experience. It is a world of "common" (or ordinary) sense, in which ways of acting and understanding are taken for granted. Our way of being in the life-world is typically characterized by the natural attitude. The natural attitude finds its expression in "benign acceptance." We, all of us, simply accept without question the hundreds of routine, seemingly unimportant activities which make up every day of our lives. I have in mind activities such as locking and unlocking doors, watching the sun rise or set, or talking on the telephone, among countless others.

The thematization of the life-world does not mean that we must actively question each and every one of our daily doings; to do so seriously would prohibit living through a single day. We need a tacit acceptance, a natural attitude, in order to cope with the daily demands on consciousness.

Reflecting on the life-world necessitates an act of withdrawal. The flow of the everyday must be interrupted. We are, of course, all familiar with what might be called customary interruptions, which occur, for example, when we accidently bump into a passerby on the street. It is but a momentary jolt, and we typically slip right back into the "harness" of the taken-for-granted. There are also ruder interruptions, which force a real disengagement from the taken-for-granted (the feeling that one has after a long airplane ride, in which two different countries, or cultures, are experienced in one day, for example). Of course, these kinds of happenings frequently provoke an intense response, since they tend to have a jolting, jarring effect. Phenomenologically, the attempt is to transform this disengagement into a "reflective grasping." A phenomenological analysis of the life-world should be an attempt to "sustain that kind of shock and disengagement systematically and then methodically to explore in depth what then is disclosed to us."[29]

To summarize, phenomenology, as an epistemology, overcomes the unwarranted adoption of physical science methods in the social sciences, and the concomitant difficulty of accounting for the active (human) observer investigating the passive (human) object of study. The relational epistemology suggested by phenomenology construes inquiry as a communicative process between subject and object, observer and observed. The concept of the life-world enables phenomenology to approach human behavior through the concrete, lived experience of social actors. For public administration theory, the concept of the life-world allows us to focus on the concrete, lived experience of administrative and organizational actors, as the best way to apprehend administrative behavior. We thus have the potential for a theory, a phenomenology of public administration, which is fundamentally concerned with the choices and problem sets confronting practicing public administrators in their day-to-day activities. This is a theory which we can teach, and one which students will seek out rather than avoid, because it must, by its very nature, inform practice.

Ideological Foundations

The ideological foundations for a teachable theory of public administration must be formulated around the concrete problem sets which face the practicing public administrator. While it is difficult at best to generalize to all administrative situations, I believe many of these problem sets can be usefully subsumed under three rubrics: context, communication, and choice. I will discuss them in order.

Social science in general and public administration in particular have emphasized analytic and deductive thinking to the severe detriment of contextual thinking. The ability to apprehend oneself in a context is a critical element of being human and is clearly essential for any future public administration. The reasons have to do with the particular context in which we find ourselves embedded at present. Before elaborating, however, I want to show what I mean by contextual thinking by quoting at length a case example made known to me by Sir Geoffrey Vickers:[30]

> In early I.Q. test days, tests briefly became an English party game. At a party our host said he would test our intelligence. He then read quickly a number of disconnected statements about three men, driver, "fireman" and guard of a (steam) railway train, whose names (but in no stated order) were Jones, Smith and Robinson. The last statement was "Smith beat the fireman at billiards." Then came the question—"What was the name of the engine driver?"
>
> The fireman's name was not Smith. But so what? There were still three possibilities for the driver. Two must have been foreclosed by some information derivable from that jumble of earlier statements but none of the statements, except the last, had specifically attributed or excluded a name to or from anyone. Nonetheless in the silence that followed, my wife immediately and confidently said "Smith."
>
> The following dialogue ensued.
>
> Host.   You mean Smith was the name of the engine driver?
>
> E.   Of course.
>
> Host.   How did you do it so quickly?
>
> E.   Do what?
>
> Host.   Solve the clues.
>
> E.   What clues?
>
> Host.   patiently but painedly explains what the clues were for.
>
> E.   Oh, I didn't understand all that.
>
> Host.   (totally puzzled) Then how did you know that the engine driver's name was Smith?

E.   (equally puzzled) But of course it would have been the engine
           driver who was playing billiards with the fireman. They work
           on the same foot plate, they belong to the same union. The
           guard is at the other end of the train, a different union, a dif-
           ferent promotion ladder. He wouldn't even know the fireman.

(A pause, broken by increasing laughter.)

Host.   He might have done.

E.   I suppose. (pause.) But Smith *was* the name of the engine driv-
           er, wasn't it?

Host.   (glumly) Yes.

To my wife an engine driver was an engine driver, a fireman a fireman. The
rest of us had thrown away all the information included in their contexts
and treated these men as symbols A, B and C. We knew what was expected
of us to show intelligence. She didn't.

The Elements of Contextual Understanding   There are, it seems to me, three
areas essential to the kind of contextual understanding needed in public administration today. The three areas are technology, organization, and ecological scarcity, and they should be construed as structural conditions of society. The centrality of each can be illustrated by the brief mention of a maj-
or work which describes the role of each in the context of public administration.

The masterwork on the role and significance of technology in modern society is still Jacques Ellul's *The Technological Society*, published in English
translation in 1964 and in the French original in 1954.[31] The sheer prescience
of the book is stunning; its theme is the essential tragedy of a civilization increasingly dominated by technique. Ellul describes what he calls the technical
imperative: "The twofold intervention of reason and consciousness in the
technical world, which produces the technical phenomenon, can be described
as the quest of the one best means in every field."[32] The technical imperative
is what distinguishes the new technique from the old. The old technique had
inherent limitations: (1) its narrow application; (2) the relative crudity of
the technique itself; (3) its local or provincial character; and (4) its slow evolution.[33] The new technique has overcome these limitations and is characterized by: (1) technical automatism—the drive for the "one best way" is auto-
matic; (2) self-augmentation—technique is irreversible and progresses geomet-
rically; (3) monolithic character—the technical phenomenon encompasses all
separate techniques and can only be understood as a whole; (4) technical un-
iversalism—technique is cross-cultural, displaces historical civilization, and

and transforms it into technical civilization, and (5) autonomy—technique conditions other aspects of civilization but is not itself conditioned by them.[34]

The last bastions of humanity, according to Ellul, are the instinctive and spiritual domains, and these are under siege by "human techniques." If these give way, as Ellul expects, we shall see the final triumph of technique:

> With the final integration of the instinctive and the spiritual by means of these human techniques, the edifice of the technical society will be completed. It will not be a universal concentration camp, for it will be guilty of no atrocity. It will not seem insane for everything will be ordered, and the stains of human passion will be lost amid the chromium gleam. We shall have nothing more to lose, and nothing to win. Our deepest instincts and our most secret passions will be analyzed, published and exploited. We shall be rewarded with everything our hearts ever desired. And the supreme luxury of the society of technical necessity will be to grant the bonus of useless revolt and of an acquiescent smile.[35]

The question for the practice of public administration is: How does one act in the face of the technical imperative?

A second important contextual element for public administration is the modern organization. The organization of course has been a strong area of study in both public administration and social science, but the focus has been largely on the internal operations of the organization. What is the contextual significance of the modern organization? A recent book, *Organizational America*, by Scott and Hart, posits an interesting answer to the question. They suggest that there is an organizational imperative operating that is characterized by two propositions and three rules. The two propositions are:[36] (1) "Whatever is good for the individual can only come from the modern organization," and (2) "Therefore, all behavior must enhance the health of such organizations." The Three rules are: (1) "The rule of technical rationality is the common denominator for all scientifically conditioned, technologically oriented organizations in advanced nations," (2) "The organizational imperative requires competent stewards whose primary loyalty must be to the organizational imperative's a priori propositions," and (3) "Pragmatic behavior enables the organization to survive in good health in changing environments, as circumstances continually impose different necessities upon managers." The organizational imperative has been acting to alter the American value system, changing the focus of concern from the individual to the organization:[37]

Individual Values	Organizational Values
From:	To:
Innate human nature	Malleability
Individuality	Obedience
Indispensability	Dispensability
Community	Specialization
Spontaneity	Planning
Volunteerism	Paternalism

The implications of this transition, according to Scott and Hart, are an ominous and perhaps irreversible drive into totalitarianism, which is seen as the ultimate realization of the organizational imperative. The value questions posed for the public administrator are serious and represent an inescapable aspect of the context which envelopes us.

Ecological scarcity represents yet another imperative looming on the horizon. William Ophuls' book, *Ecology and the Politics of Scarcity*, offers a comprehensive treatment of the dimensions of this problem. The basic message is simple enough: We are leaving an age of aberrant abundance in human history and returning to the historical norm of scarcity. The concomitant limitations will (or already have in some cases) manifest themselves in the areas of population, food, mineral resources, pollution, energy, and the management of technology. This message is painful, as evidenced by the blatant and thoroughgoing avoidance behavior with which we have so far confronted it. Ophuls summarizes the essential message of ecology as follows:

> . . . although it is possible in principle to exploit nature rationally and reasonably for human ends, man has not done so. Because he has not been content with the portion naturally allotted him, man has invaded the biological capital built up by evolution. . . . With our new ecological understanding, we can see that linear, single-purpose exploitation of nature is not in harmony with the laws of the biosphere and must be abandoned . . . for the essential message of ecology is *limitation*: there is only so much the biosphere can take and only so much it can give, and this may be less than we desire.[38]

He goes on to suggest a politics of the steady state that differs considerably
from our present political and economic institutions, yet which seems abso-
lutely necessary if we are to cope with these inexorable limits. Geoffrey Vickers summarizes the dilemma as follows:

> Relying on automatic regulation, the countries of the West, over the last
> two hundred years, have built a political and economic system far beyond
> their capacity to regulate by conscious intervention. Yet they have increas-
> ing evidence that it is not self-sustaining and that the only "automatic" reg-
> ulators which might "stabilize" it at any level, however remote from its   •
> present one, are war, famine and pestilence, of which the first two are al-
> ready much in evidence. Efforts to combine automatic with deliberate reg-
> ulation, even within the frontiers of individual western states, have generated
> disappointment and resistance. . . . [39]

Responding to this dilemma requires a simultaneous, if somewhat schizophren-
ic, ability to understand and act on (1) ever larger, more complicated, and
interconnected systems and (2) smaller scale, more human, more manageable
systems. We need both much more coupling (our first response to the dilemma) and much more decoupling (our second response) than we now have. The
coupling needed is in greater part psychological (as in apprehending the planet
as "spaceship earth"), whereas the decoupling needed seems in larger part fac-
tual (as in decentralizing the provision of goods and services to the point where
people have a greater degree of freedom in choosing their constraints and
commitments).

Ecological scarcity, organization, and technology are constituents making
up a very difficult, if not wholly intractable, context within which public administration must occur. To practice public administration in any way other
than in the light of this context would be folly. Any theory of public administration must, therefore, adequately represent this context.

Communication as Praxis   The second element in the ideological foundation of
a teachable theory of public administration is communication. Communication is another of those concepts that has already seen considerable attention
in the literature, particularly as organizational communication. However, here
I want to discuss communication, communicative interaction, as praxis. Praxis is often characterized as theoretically informed communicative interaction,
and, as such, represents an important step beyond simple practice. When we
focus narrowly on practice, we take a fundamentally conservative attitude;
our orientation is toward what we have done in the past, toward retention.
Our possibilities for action are bound and circumscribed. Praxis, on the other

hand, allows one to consider explicitly the theoretical dimension, which is present, but usually implicit, in all forms of practice. Praxis permits, then, a consideration of future possibilities, of protention; we become able to address directly the tensions and ambiguities inherent in the human context.

The idea of praxis as communicative interaction has been developed at some length and sophistication in the work of Jürgen Habermas, the German critical theorist. He contrasts praxis with "techne," systems of purposive-rational action (the same functional rationality which I argued earlier underpins current public administration ideology). Techne is a limited sort of action, restricted to the rational implementation of techniques or strategies (and hence closely related to the technical and organizational imperatives).

The domain of praxis, an alternative, broader sphere of action, refers not to purposive-rational action, but to communicative interaction. Table 1 illustrates these two domains of action, praxis and techne, whose relation Habermas characterizes as the distinction, "between (1) the *institutional framework* of a society or the sociocultural life-world and (2) the subsystems of *purposive-rational action* that are 'embedded' in it."[40]

In developing further his ideas on communicative interation, or praxis, Habermas introduced the idea of communicative competence, in which everyday language is based on the expectation of a consensus achievable through nonrepressive discourse, or discourse free of domination—ideal speech. It is argued that language rests on a background consensus of four claims: (1) that it is understandable; (2) that its propositional content is true; (3) that the speaker is sincere; and (4) that it is right or appropriate for the particular speaker to be performing the speech act in question.[41] This leads Habermas to put forward the notion of "systematically distorted communication," as descriptive of the structural conditions of modern society. In modern society, praxis—communicative interaction—finds itself in a degenerative relation to techne, a relation in which communication is systematically distorted. A focus on communication, praxis, as a part of the ideological foundation for public administration theory prods us to expose systematic distortions of communication and to strive for ways to achieve communicative competence. I believe communicative competence can only be achieved through democracy, the essence of which I take to be interactive discourse among equals with the aim of building community. I would agree with John Dewey's characterization of democracy as "a name for a life of free and enriching communion.
. . . It will have its consummation when free social inquiry is indissolubly wedded to the art of full and moving communication."[42] I would also agree with Mary Parker Follett's view of democracy as "the bringing forth of a genuine collective will, one to which every single being must contribute the whole of

Table 1 Praxis and Techne

	Praxis: Institutional framework: communicative interaction	Techne: Systems of purposive-rational (instrumental and strategic) action
Action-orienting rules	Social norms	Technical rules
Level of definition	Intersubjectivity, shared ordinary language	Context-free language
Type of definition	Reciprocal expectations about behavior	Conditional predictions, conditional imperatives
Mechanism of acquisition	Role internalization	Learning of skills and qualifications
Function of action type	Maintenance of institutions (conformity to norms on the basis of reciprocal enforcement)	Problem solving (goal attainment, defined in means-ends relations)
Sanctions against violations of rules	Punishment on the basis of conventional sanctions: failure against authority	Inefficacy: failure in reality
"Rationalization"	Emancipation, individuation; extension of communication free of domination	Growth of productive forces; extension of power of technical control

Source: Adapted from *Toward a Rational Society* by Jürgen Habermas.
© 1970 by Beacon Press. Reprinted by permission of Beacon Press (see Ref. 40).

his complex life . . . . Thus, the essence of democracy is creating."[43] Attention to communication, praxis, leads in the direction of democratic systems, which seek to enlarge the possibilities for people to make choices for themselves.

Responsible Choice I would suggest that choice, individual and collective, is the basic administrative act. Within public administration, I would suggest that administrative praxis be viewed as choice, which forms the last leg of our ideological foundation. However, choice, like communication, is in a systematically distorted condition. Chris Argyris argues that threatening issues in organizations are "undiscussable" and, furthermore, that their undiscussability is itself undiscussable.[44] Walter Kaufmann, in his *Without Guilt or Justice: From Decidophobia to Autonomy,* notes a similar situation when difficult choices arise:

> ... comparing fateful alternatives and choosing between them with one's eyes open, fully aware of the risks, is what frightens the decidophobe. Basically, he has three options: to avoid fateful decisions; to stack the cards so that one alternative is clearly the right one, and there seems to be no risk involved at all; and to decline responsibility. . . . In brief, avoid, if possible; if that does not work, stack; and in any case make sure that you do not stand alone.[45]

Overcoming decidophobia enables one to achieve autonomy, that is, the ability to choose responsibly. The ideal is for the individual to be free to choose her or his own commitments and constraints. The reality is that the context within which we find ourselves has certain "requirednesses."[46] Choosing responsibly within public administration, then, may mean no more, and no less, than choosing those commitments and constraints which are required of us. Some further guidance in our choices comes from Geoffrey Vickers:

> I have personally a hope, though only a hope, not quite a faith, that there is to be seen in human history what I would call a trans-cultural vector, a direction in which in any given context, it is most human or least inhuman to move. One of the near-imperatives of this view is the importance of raising the level of trust and the quality (no, not the quantity) of human communication.[47]

The tasks of administrative praxis, making responsible choices, seem both clear and formidable.

Choice, communication, and context I believe, offer a strong, ideological foundation for an adequate theory of public administration. That theory must of course include elements of "techne," of functional rationalization, but, as that aspect has dominated the field, it need not be more than mentioned.

I have argued here that the theories in use in public administration education are for all practical purposes unteachable. These theories fail on both epistemological and ideological grounds. A teachable theory, one that integrates process and content to facilitate the growth of the learner, can be developed through a coherent integration of adequate epistemological (process) and ideological (content) founcations. If such a theory can be elaborated from the skeleton offered here, I believe that the practice of public administration would be better informed and that the public service could become socially valuable in a way that it presently is not.

Notes

1. Waldo, D. *The Enterprise of Public Administration*. Chandler and Sharp, Novato, Calif., 1980, pp. 173–186.
2. For example, management techniques (management by objectives), budgeting techniques (zero-base budgeting), organization development techniques (team building), etc.
3. I base this observation on a broad familiarity with public administration curricula around the country. No report on public administration education that I have seen even uses public administration theory as a course category.
4. Denhardt, R. B. and Denhardt, K. G. Public Administration and the Critique of Domination. *Administration and Society II* (May, 1979):107–120.
5. Fay, B. *Social Theory and Political Practice*. Allen and Unwin, London, 1976, p. 13.
6. Bernstein, R. J. *Restructuring Social and Political Theory*. Harcourt, Brace, Jovanovich, New York, 1976, pp. 11–16, *passim*.
7. *Ibid*, Part I.
8. *Ibid*, pp. 26–27.
9. Natanson, M. Phenomenology and the social sciences: introduction in *Phenomenology and the Social Sciences*. Northwestern University Press, Evanston, Ill., 1973, pp. 42–43.
10. Geertz, C. *The Interpretation of Cultures*. Basic Books, New York, 1975, p. 25.
11. The problems of using concepts and theories from other disciplines are discussed ably in an article on "misplacement." See Guerreiro-Ramos, A. Misplacement of Concepts and Administrative Theory. *Public Administration Review 38* (November-December, 1978):550–556.
12. Mannheim, K. *Man and Society in an Age of Reconstruction*. Harcourt, Brace and World, New York, 1940, pp. 51–60.
13. Horkheimer, M. *The Eclipse of Reason*. Oxford University Press, New York, 1947.
14. Bay, C. From contract to community: thoughts on liberalism and post-industrial society, in Dallmayr, F. (ed.), *From Contract to Community*. Marcel Dekker, New York, 1980, p. 35.

15. Macpherson, C. B. The false roots of western democracy, in Dallmayr, F. (ed.), *From Contract to Community.* Marcel Dekker, New York, 1980, pp. 22–23.
16. Bay, *From Contract to Community,* p. 30.
17. Frederickson, G. The lineage of new public administration, in Bellone, C. J. (ed.), *Organization Theory and the New Public Administration.* Allyn and Bacon, Boston, 1980.
18. Weinstein, J. *The Corporate Ideal in the Liberal State: 1900–1918.* Beacon Press, Boston, 1968.
19. See, for example, Becker, C. *Freedom and Responsibility in the American Way of Life.* Little, Brown, Boston, 1960; Girvetz, H. *The Evolution of Liberalism.* Collier, New York, 1963; Grimes, A. P. *American Political Thought.* Holt, Rinehart and Winston, New York, 1966; and Hartz, L. M. *The Liberal Tradition in America.* Harcourt, Brace, Jovanovich, New York, 1955.
20. Fay, Social Theory and Political Practice, p. 71.
21. *Ibid.*
22. *Ibid,* p. 80.
23. See Freire, P. *Education for Critical Consciousness.* Seabury Press, New York, 1973; and Shor, I. *Critical Teaching and Everyday Life.* South End Press, Boston, 1980.
24. White, O., Jr. Introduction: Toward a Grounded Approach to Public Administration Education. *Southern Review of Public Administration 3* (December 1979):253–263.
25. See, for example, Husserl, E. *Ideas.* Collier, New York, 1962; idem, *The Crisis of European Sciences and Transcendental Phenomenology.* Northwestern University Press, Evanston, Ill., 1970.
26. Most notably Paul Ricoeur, Martin Heidegger, and Hans-Georg Gadamer.
27. Husserl, *The Crisis,* p. 143.
28. Natanson, M. The nature of social man, in Edie, J. M., Parker, F. M., and Schrag, C. O. (eds.) *Patterns of the Life-World.* Northwestern University Press, Evanston, Ill., 1970.
29. Zaner, R. *The Way of Phenomenology.* Pegasus Books, New York, 1970, p. 56.
30. Vickers, Sir G. Personal correspondence, September 14, 1979.
31. Ellul, J. *The Technological Society.* Vintage Books, New York, 1964.
32. *Ibid,* p. 21.
33. *Ibid,* pp. 64–65.
34. *Ibid,* pp. 79–147, *passim.*
35. *Ibid,* p. 427.
36. Scott, W. G. and Hart, D. K. *Organizational America.* Houghton-Mifflin, Boston, 1980, pp. 43–45.

37. *Ibid,* p. 54.
38. Ophuls, W. *Ecology and the Politics of Scarcity.* W. H. Freeman, San Francisco, 1977, p. 43.
39. Vickers, Sir G. *Responsibility: Its Sources and Limits.* Intersystems, Seaside, Calif., 1980, p. 119.
40. Habermas, J. *Toward a Rational Society.* Beacon Press, Boston, 1970, p. 94.
41. McCarthy, T. Translator's introduction, in Habermas, J. *Legitimation Crisis.* Beacon Press, Boston, 1975, p. xviii.
42. Dewey, J. *The Public and Its Problems.* Swallow Press, Chicago, 1927, p. 184.
43. Follett, M. P. *The New State.* Longman, Green and Co., New York, 1918, p. 7.
44. Argyris, C. Making the Undiscussable and Its Undiscussability Discussable. *Public Administration Review 40* (May–June, 1980):205–213.
45. Kaufmann, W. *Without Guilt or Justice: From Decidophobia to Autonomy.* Delta Books, New York, 1973, p. 4.
46. Vickers, *Responsibility,* p. 33.
47. Ibid., p. 8.

9
Careers in Public Administration Education

James F. Wolf
Virginia Polytechnic Institute and State University, Falls Church, Virginia

The growth in public administration education programs has paralleled the increase in professional education in general. Universities offering traditional professional degrees, MBA, MPA, MSW, etc., have all expanded their programs dramatically over the past two decades. As university programs increase, the need for a workforce of public administration educators also grows. Furthermore, as the public administration field matures, demands for more specialized facilities complicates workforce planning and staffing patterns.

Understanding the nature of the public administration education career environment is clearly essential for those who have chosen it as their career field. Individuals in doctoral programs are already making long-term occupational investments and commitments. For many others, a switch to public administration education after a successful tenure in management practice represents an important second career option. No matter how or where the career is chosen, however, the questions about public administration education—opportunities and constraints, the supply and nature of the clientele, and the existing and potential workforce—remain to be answered.

A public management education workforce is also important to those concerned with the direction of public administration education. Most people in teaching roles are not there purely by accident. They have attained their positions because of certain experiences, degrees, interests, competencies, and contacts. Their orientation to public service and the nature of public administration education is to a great extent based on these career socialization experiences. Their views about the nature and role of the public servant are a significant force in determining the overall quality of the public sector. Mosher's argument that professional education in the "professional state" is central to preserving certain kinds of political values and orientation to public action is a cogent statement of the reason for concern about public administration education.[1]

This chapter attempts to address the question of the nature of public administration education careers. It does so with the occupational environment in mind and from the perspective of the individual public administration educator. At the occupational environment level, the relevant issues addressed include: the current scope of university-based public administration education programs, the size of the teaching workforce, the academic setting, program missions, and the perceived status among the universities. An exploration of the individual's career experience in public administration education includes a look at career paths, role identities, and career anchors. Finally, issues that confront individuals as they seek to enter this career field are examined.

The Career Environment

The occupational market for public administration education careers cannot be easily defined. Education in public management occurs in a variety of contexts, and most such activities occur outside formal university degree programs. On-the-job training experiences, agency and university institutes, and private entrepreneurs offer a wide range of public management training and education. These efforts were given impetus at the federal level by the Government Employees Training Act, the Intergovernmental Personnel Act, and an increasing number of other federally funded training for special programs. Although a catalog of these activities and a description of the occupational market of training and education in such programs are beyond the scope of the chapter, it is important to recognize them as an important part of public management education.

This chapter focuses on the occupational roles (jobs) located at universities with degree-granting programs including: MPA and MS, earned doctorates in public administration and public affairs (Ph.D. and DPA) and, to a lesser extent, undergraduate programs in public management.

The Scope of the Demand for Public Administration Education Services

There are currently an estimated 220 academic institutions in the United States that offer degrees in public management and administration or public affairs. Of these, 185 responded to the 1979 survey of member institutions of NASPAA.[2] The surveys represent the level of growth in public administration programs.[3-5] In the 1973 survey, only 101 institutions were represented. In 1979, 185 responded. At the same time, graduate program enrollments rose from 19,731 in 1973 to 28,252 in 1979. The growth between 1977 and 1979 alone was 13 percent. There were also an estimated 13,820 undergraduates in public affairs and administration programs in 1979.

To a significant degree the nature of the student population in public administration programs molds professional public administration education. The students are overwhelmingly part time (63%), mid-career (75%), and off campus (73%). Thus, the typical student may be a 35-year-old, mid-career adult taking an evening class as part of an MPA program in a downtown location away from a university campus.

Degrees granted during this period provide an indication of the market for services that public administration education offer. Degrees are primarily at the master's level with a small but significant increase in earned doctorates. Between 1973 and 1979, the number of advanced degrees increased from 2,907 to over 6,300, a more than two-fold increase (See Table 1).

The major growth during the eight-year period represented by Table 1 has been at the master's level. However, the 1977 to 1979 data suggest some possible new trends. First, the growth of master's level education has slowed. This stabilization of the market seems to be a response to several forces including: tighter public budgets, a demise of federal programs (e.g., the Law Enforcement Assistance Administration, or LEAA) that traditionally have been important supporters of master's level education, saturation of MPA markets in certain metropolitan areas, and the recent no-growth status of state and local and now national government employment. The number of potential public sector in-career managers is finite, and as these forces come into play, demand for the MPAs will slow.

Another trend indicated by Table 1 is the increased variety of master's degrees with public management components. More business administration,

Table 1 Public Administration/Affairs Graduate Degrees Awarded
1973–1979

Degrees	1973	1975	1977	1979
Masters (MPA, MS, MA, MUA)	2,707	4,586	6,049	5,791
Ph.D./DPA	150	131	161	199
Others	N/A	N/A	400	853
Total	2,857	5,592	6,616	6,843

Source: Data from surveys published in NASPAA Directories for the years 1974, 1976,
1978, and 1980.

social science, and general management programs now offer public affairs- and
public administration-related degrees. Sometimes these specialized or hybrid
degrees are the only variety able to survive the university political process. In
other cases, there is an intentional decision to offer specialized emphasis in a
related professional degree.

The career market also shows a slow but significant increase in earned doctorates. The 1979 data may not sufficiently reflect this growth because a number of DPA programs are new and do not yet have degree candidates. But both
Ph.D. and DPA degree graduates have increased. The DPA is seen as an attractive alternative for practitioners because it offers postmaster's education and
an earned doctorate. It can increase opportunities for career movement in a
current career and in alternative roles such as researcher, consultant, and
teacher. The Ph.D. is still, however, the principal degree required for those
seeking teaching roles and is also valuable in certain practitioner fields. Part
of the data for the doctorates awarded in 1979 somewhat distorts the growth
of the degree. NOVA University of Fort Lauderdale, with nine full-time
faculty, has awarded 31 percent of all earned doctorates throughout the
country (62 of 199). Their DPA degree is nontraditional and their requirements and orientation differ from other doctoral programs.

In sum, the market for public administration teaching has grown considerably in the last 10 years, but there are indications of stabilization. There are also suggestions of a small but growing demand for the DPA or postmaster's work. This latter trend may be particularly apparent in areas where government is an important industry and a large number of managers already have master's degrees. Washington, D.C., Los Angeles, and several state capitals are probable areas of growth for postmaster's work.

Size of the Public Administration Education Workforce

Though hard numbers are difficult to come by, the 1979 NASPAA report offers some indication of the scale of the public administration education labor force. The analysis presented below in Table 2 was based on a random sample of 50 out of the 185 institutions that responded to the NASPAA survey.

An estimated regular faculty in excess of 5000 teach in the 185 programs. An estimated 1350 faculty members (24%) are designated as being from the "field" of public administration. The second largest group, approximately 900 (16% of total), are political science faculty teaching in public administration programs. The majority of this group teach in a political science department from which the public administration degree is offered. The next largest group comes from economics faculties. The remaining 2600 (46%) of the regular faculty in PA programs come from a variety of disciplines, with the greatest number from business administration and planning fields. Other disciplines represented are: statistics, computer science, urban affairs, sociology, psychology, health, law, social work, engineering, history, geography, and criminal justice, in that general order.

This teaching faculty in public administration programs then is clearly an interdisciplinary group. It consists of a large core of public administration and political science types surrounded by a host of related disciplines in social sciences and special program areas. This mix may present problems for clarity of program purpose, but offers an opportunity for a variety of professional orientations within PA programs.

The size of the *full-time faculty* in public administration programs, however, is substantially smaller than 5000. Based on the sample of 50 schools in the survey, there are over 1000 full-time faculty engaged in the public administration and public affairs programs. The mode for the full-time faculty in a program is 4, whereas the average is 5.4 (see Table 3). The full-time faculty are being substantially supported by an additional 1100 part-time instructors

Table 2 Regular Faculty in Public Administration/Affairs Programs (1980)

	Regular Faculty by Fields				
Number of faculty in programs	Public adminis- tration N (%)	Political science N (%)	Economics N (%)	Other N (%)	PA/A faculty N (%)
0–2	14 (28)	15 (30	32 (64)	3 (6)	0 (0)
3–5	17 (34)	23 (46)	10 (20)	10 (20)	0 (0)
6–10	10 (20)	9 (18)	6 (12)	13 (26)	6 (12)
11–15	4 (8)	1 (2)	1 (2)	6 (12)	8 (16)
16–20	3 (6)	1 (2)	0 (0)	7 (14)	9 (18)
21–30	2 (4)	0 (0)	1 (2)	7 (14)	11 (22)
31 +	0 (0)	1 (2)	0 (0)	4 (8)	16 (32)
Total	50 (100)	50 (100)	50 (100)	50 (100)	50 (100)
Average size by field	7.3	4.9	3.0	14.5	29.7
Estimated total by field faculty for 185 programs	1350	966	555	2682	5494

Source: Data is based on random sample of 50 of 185 programs reported in 1980 NASPAA Directory.

along with the 3500 faculty from other departments at the colleges and universities.

Although 140 earned doctorates, excluding those awarded by NOVA University, are added each year to the supply of potential academics, not all of them will be university teachers. Many of those who receive the DPA remain practitioners or teach in programs other than public administration. The same options exist for those who receive a Ph.D. degree, but a greater percentage choose academic roles. Assuming that the turnover of the workforce is in the neighborhood of 10 percent per year, the current production of doctorates for teaching occupations is slightly shy of meeting the demands for new faculty.

This production deficit accounts for the fact that many positions within public administration faculties are filled by those holding doctorates from other programs.

Academic Setting

The institutional setting and organizational arrangement of a public administration program is a critical factor in PA education career options. These organizational arrangements affect faculty recruitment, selection, promotion, and tenure decisions. In most instances, teaching positions are filled through departmental selection committees, collegial groups which have a major influence on recruitment, selection, promotion, and granting of tenure. Each faculty tends to represent its own discipline or field interest in these processes. Whether the program is based on a particular discipline, such as economics or public administration, the interplay of particular interests influences career opportunities and career movement.

There are a variety of configurations in public administration/affairs programs, many of which are simply the result of historical accident or power

Table 3 Full-time Faculty in PA/A Programs

Number of full-time faculty in programs	N	%
0–2	15	30
3–5	20	40
6–10	9	18
11–15	2	4
16–20	1	1
21+	3	6
Total	50	100
Average faculty size	5.4	—
Estimated total for 185 programs	999	—

Source: Data from 1980 NASPAA Directory

politics. Table 4 describes the general organizational arrangements of PA programs.

Most early public administration programs began as a section of a political science department, and this arrangement is still a dominant organizational form. Over the period 1973 to 1979, about 37 percent of all PA programs have remained in political science departments. When the MPA is the dominant degree in the political science department, the public administration program and faculty usually have a major influence in decision making and are able to successfully represent a professional and "practice" orientation. In many other instances, however, the public administration program is a stepchild of the political science department. The traditional tension over the

Table 4 Organizational Patterns of PA/A Programs

Organizational Pattern	1973	1975	1977	1979
1. Separate professional schools	25 (25%)	29 (25%)	32 (20%)	29 (15%)
2. Separate departments in large unit	23 (22.5%)	35 (25%)	49 (31%)	64 (34%)
3. PA/A program combined with another professional school or department (e.g., business adm.)	17 (16.5%)	22 (16%)	16 (10%)	20 (10%)
4. PA/A program within political science	26 (36%)	52 (37%)	62 (39%)	70 (37%)
5. Unclassified department	–	–	–	8 (4%)
Total	101 (100%)	138 (100%)	156 (100%)	185 (100%)

Source: Data from the 1974, 1976, 1978, and 1980 NASPAA Directories

issue of "the legitimate role of public administration" in political science is prevalent in these circumstances. The bias of the political science discipline frequently places the practice orientation of public administration in a secondary role. The PA program may be helpful in increasing student count, but it remains an unfortunate irritant to many political science faculty. Most PA programs within political science departments are a product of history and necessity and not one of intention by either the political science or the public administration communities.

Separate Public Administration Departments and Schools. Nearly half of the programs in public administration in the NASPAA survey are autonomous departments or separate schools of public administration and affairs. Separate departments increased from 23 percent in 1973 to over 34 percent of all reporting institutions in 1979. These departments frequently have a core PA faculty and have academic positions fully staffed from other professional disciplines—most frequently, business administration, operations and research organization behavior, and economics and finance. The professional orientation is likely to be diverse with the American Society for Public Administration (ASPA) serving as the predominant professional organization. Fifteen percent of all public administration programs are offered in professional schools of that discipline. These schools are often the larger and older of the university programs. The schools at the universities of Southern California, Indiana, and Colorado, Harvard, Princeton, New York University, and the University of Pittsburgh are examples of such professional schools. Within the school, departments and subfaculties are separated.

The remaining public administration programs are typically combined with another professional degree program, for example, business administration and management. Because of the larger market for the MBA degrees, the public management programs tend to have problems similar to those within political science departments. The norms and status systems of combined programs tend to be those of the business administration orientation.

Programmatic Mission

Although these public administration programs share certain objectives, they often have different operating mandates. Most programs are primarily teaching schools. They may emphasize either the preservice full-time student or the part-time in-career student. Those that cater to pre-entry full-time students have low faculty/student ratios and small enrollments, and move students through programs in groups. These programs are characteristic of those found in political science departments. The University of North Carolina and the University of Kansas are representative of these programs.

Other teaching schools seek their clientele in the part-time, in-career student. They are typically located in larger metropolitan markets and have high student/faculty ratios. In the California State University-Long Beach program, for example, 225 of 250 students are part time. At Suffolk University in Boston, 151 of the 190 students are part time and at mid-career levels. The full-time faculty may be expected to write and research but often find that the teaching, counseling, and program management demands drive out these activities. Some programs that cater to the part-time, in-career student offer services at off-campus locations some distance from the main university, often at defense installations or major urban centers. A small administrative staff at the base or metropolitan center will organize and provide student services, while the core faculty commute to the off-campus locations or are local practitioners.

A limited group of "comprehensive" programs offer master's and doctoral programs for full- and part-time students, provide consulting and training programs, and expect significant research efforts by the faculty. Though small in number, such schools produce most of the faculties for other public administration programs. In 1979, the University of Southern California, New York University, Pittsburgh, George Washington, Carnegie-Mellon, Syracuse, Georgia, and SUNY-Albany produced 86 of the 199 doctorates in public administration and public affairs.

Status Among Programs

Another important dimension in the public administration education career environment is the differential status of programs. However unjust and inaccurate, perceptions of status differentials influence career opportunities. A potential faculty member can expect that a higher status institution will give him or her greater mobility than would one with a perceived lower status. Popular wisdom dictates that one can move easily from a higher status to a lower status institution but that it is far more difficult to move in the reverse direction. In late 1980, a NASPAA survey asked program directors to rank the top 10 public administration and public affairs programs in the United States. The 25 schools scoring highest are listed in Table 5.

Such lists are always fraught with problems. Reputations lag behind the changes in programs. An improved program gains status slowly, while a program that loses some of its quality loses its reputation even more slowly. Many regional schools and newer programs are currently making major investments in recruiting quality faculty and in upgrading their services and research

Table 5 Ranking of top 25 Public Administration/Public Policy Programs by
NASPÁA principal representatives

School	First Place Votes	Total Points	School	First Place Votes	Total Points
1. Syracuse	28	770	14. American	1	114
2. Harvard	25	668	15. North Carolina		110
3. Southern California	22	592	16. Florida State		95
4. Indiana	12	482	17. Kansas		93
5. California-Berkeley	5	334	18. George Washington		77
6. Texas	2	331	19. Virginia Polytech		69
7. Princeton	4	264	20. SUNY-Albany		68
8. Pittsburgh	2	251	21. Columbia		64
9. Michigan	2	241	22. New York University		63
10. Georgia	4	225	23. Northwestern		63
11. Carnegie Mellon	2	151	24. Wisconsin		62
12. Minnesota		121	25. Colorado		54
13. Ohio State	1	119			

Note: The tabulations represent the usable responses of 118 NASPAA principal representatives (55 percent of the total) to a questionnaire mailed in the fall of 1980 asking for
their perceptions of the top 10 public administration/public policy graduate programs in
the United States. 118 responses from NASPAA principal representatives: Total points
based on 10 points for first place and 9 points for second place, etc.

Source: From note 6.

activities. In the near future, many of these newer programs can be expected
to supplant or rival the current high-status programs.

The Individual Career

While occupational and workforce issues, as outlined in the foregoing para-
graphs, define and constrain the careers of those in public administration

education, each person's career is unique. Attention to the career from the individual's perspective is important in public administration education because of the heterogeneous and diffused character of the career structure. No single entry point or route to success exists. Each individual, therefore, plays an even more important role in defining the nature of this career. The career is circumscribed by the demand for teaching personnel, specialization of teaching roles within public administration programs, and the status of the person seeking success in the career. Beyond these constraints, career movement is in the hands of the individual creating the career. This section explores ways in which a person in public administration education creates and makes sense of the career experience.

Career Paths

A person can approach a public administration teaching role from several different directions. There are four general paths, however, that characterize movement into and through a public administration teaching career: the life-long academic, the second careerist, the bimodal path, and the part-timer.

The *life-long academic* route represents the typical academic career. A person in this career completes graduate school immediately after receiving the bachelor's degree. At this point he or she begins at the bottom of the academic ladder as an assistant professor or instructor, moves on to associate, and then full professor, using the tenure time clock established by the American Association of University Professors. The life-long academic career path may include a brief practice period. The NASPAA Fellows Program is one vehicle for providing a one-year experience in the federal government. Someone in this path would most likely see their professional identity as closely tied to the standard academic career modal.

Because public administration has a practice orientation, many public managers with significant administrative or policy-making experiences make the career transition to public administration education. The *second careerist* normally received a Ph.D. or DPA during a first career and then uses the degree to make the transition. Not all second careerists see themselves as making a major career change; rather, they view themselves as public administrators in the practice arena first, with teaching and research roles as secondary options. As demands for teachers with practical experience increase, the second career path is a viable option for many managers.

The *bimodal career* path is represented by the person who moves back and forth between academic and administrative roles. For some, this career modality represents intentional career planning. For others, the back and forth movement simply happens as a result of being successful in one area and being sought in the other. Certain careerists are able to remain attractive to both role systems and may find themselves alternating between practice and teaching several times during their career lives.

Between 1972 and 1977, the growth rate for the part-time teacher category in institutions of higher education was 50 percent, while the rate for full-time teachers was only 9 percent. This rate differential suggests that universities are increasingly using part-time academics as an important component of their delivery system. In some programs, part-time teachers play a central role. If they stay with a program over a series of years they can have a significant, part-time career. A part-time teaching career can be an attractive alternative to the routine of management and policy roles. It offers stimulation and forces one to keep up-to-date in the field. It also provides opportunities to interact with professionals outside the practice organization. Part-time teaching is also used as a transition from the role of practitioner to a second career as a full-time teacher. The experience can also be short-lived, incremental, and fragmented. A practitioner might be called in to teach a course one year and not asked to teach again for three or four years.

Job Role Identities

The way individuals perceive themselves in a career is influenced by their specific position and responsibilities. Role identities are framed by activities which they perform and the disciplines from which they are expected to teach. Like any organizational enterprise, professional education programs offer a variety of role opportunities. The predominant roles are teaching, counseling, research and writing, in-service training, and management of education programs and projects. The specific mix of such activities varies from individual to individual and from program to program. Teaching institutions obviously emphasize the teaching and counseling roles with some program management from time to time. For the academic in a "flagship" institution, the pressure is to adopt the role of scholar committed to research and writing.

In addition to institutional expectations, personal expertise helps to define role identity. The discipline labels of this expertise are public administration/ public management, public policy studies which are heavily anchored in political science, and/or the policy sciences that blend economics and political science. At the same time a person may be role-identified by subspecialty interests such as personnel, budgeting, labor relations, planning, organization behavior, organization theory, comparative administration, and normative theories. Individuals will frequently view themselves as being specialists in several of these disciplines or field areas.

Another dimension of the public administration educator's role identity may be defined by connection to a program or focus in the public arena. Topics such as housing, urban development, energy, and national security are examples of this type of orientation. Academic programs can be built around these program and policy study areas. Interest in such areas tends to ebb and flow, depending on the urgency with which they are viewed by public decision makers. As resources are directed toward a particular programmatic problem and new occupational opportunities are developed, the demand for the program focus will increase. Practitioners seeking a second career in teaching can often attain teaching positions by presenting themselves as having experience and expertise in one or another of these public concerns.

Career Anchors

Through graduate education and professional role experiences, personal skills, interests, and values combine to create public administration education career themes. These themes or anchors[7] become important forces; they help define the meaning of the career as well as guide its future direction. Schein's research on career anchors focused on managerial and technical roles. His concepts, however, can be extrapolated to the public administration occupation. Based on this writer's experience, there are at least six different anchors that describe these extrapolated career themes. These themes are: the technical functional competence, education manager, entrepreneur, autonomous academic, stable careerist, and service.

Technical Functional Competence Schein discovered that many managers seek to develop a special competence in their career. They want to become increasingly effective and specialized in a particular area. Opportunities to develop this competence define the way a person will evaluate a career. This drive to become increasingly effective at something can be fulfilled in an academic career by emphasizing a specialty within a field or discipline. Writing and research activities are often the primary vehicles for attaining a personal sense of career success.

The Education Manager For the person whose career theme is education management it is important to take on increasing responsibilities for managing educational programs. This person will probably recognize the importance of developing a skilled specialty, for instance, writing and researching, and will also teach. He or she is likely, however, to be attracted to and seek out general education management roles: chairperson of a department, deanship or other administrative positions in universities.

The Entrepreneur To the entrepreneur, building something of one's own is a central career thrust, and this individual will seek opportunities to take an idea and to create from it a new program, curriculum, or organizational context. A person with this career anchor will often get something up and going, and then move onto yet another project creation.

The Autonomous Academic A person with this anchor wants to be free from organizational constraints and frequently finds life in complex systems to be restrictive, irrational, and intrusive.[8] In public administration education, this individual may seek autonomy by taking on several roles without becoming heavily invested in any one set of role imperatives. He or she might accept teaching, research, and consulting, as well as outside professional activities in order to play these role demands against each other. Frequently a person avoids the routine of teaching courses by becoming involved with a grant or special project. By periodically emphasizing different roles, greater flexibility is possible in the total career role space.

The Stable Careerist Many times, a person will enter an academic career and seek to invest in a single organization or program. The purpose of this investment is to be surrounded by as reasonably predictable an environment as possible. Staying with the same university because of the desirable location of the campus could be an important element in the career.

Service Another attraction of the academic teaching career can be the opportunity to provide service to others on a one-to-one basis. Counseling and teaching activities are the main features of the career. The interpersonal emphasis would lead a person to find a position which emphasizes the teaching and counseling mission. Research institutions are unlikely to meet the needs of a person who has developed this service anchor.

Public Management Education Careers in the Future

The present and immediate future of the public administration education environment can be characterized as moving in several important directions.

1. The student population will stabilize and become increasingly in-career as the baby boom generation moves beyond the college-age years and public employment levels off.
2. Although career paths and occupational opportunities do exist, their structure is diffused and diverse.

3. The field is maturing and more specialized competencies in programmatic and discipline areas will increase.

Several important issues are suggested by these emerging forces.

Devising Strategies for Career Options

Operating in a heterogeneous and diffused career environment offers maximum personal career opportunity. The faculty member in public administration is not defined only by the major academic promotion route. He or she can have multiple role identities that provide career options. Such flexibility permits greater career security including movement between the practice and academic environments. A public administrator educator has potential in at least three career clusters which build a person's collective experiences, competencies, and strengths, and provide multiple opportunities by emphasizing different components of a person's career. These career clusters can be termed an *academic cluster,* a *field specialty,* and an *organizational cluster* (see Figure 1).

The academic teaching career cluster is represented by the traditional route from instructor to full professor, through the tenure process. Mobility among institutions is based on the status of earned degrees and the quality of research and publications. The basic decision in an academic career is whether to emphasize the teaching mission characteristic of regional teaching schools or to go the route that emphasizes research and writing.

The second career cluster is related to the specialty or practical competency that the public administration educator has developed. For example, individuals who see themselves in the organization behavior and organization change area can maintain creditability for career movement as organization development consultants, managers of human resource programs, or directors of training institutes. Maintaining currency through writing/research and consulting sustains the individual in the academic community and keeps open options for movement into practice.

The third career cluster that a public administrator might entertain is a career within a university, with university administration the obvious possibility. Deanships, directorships, and so forth, as well as mainline academic management of the institution, are viable career options.

Theory and Practice Role Tension

Sustaining the tension between the world of practice and the world of theory is a central challenge for public administration education. This is imperative because the field is one of relating theory to practice and practice to theory,

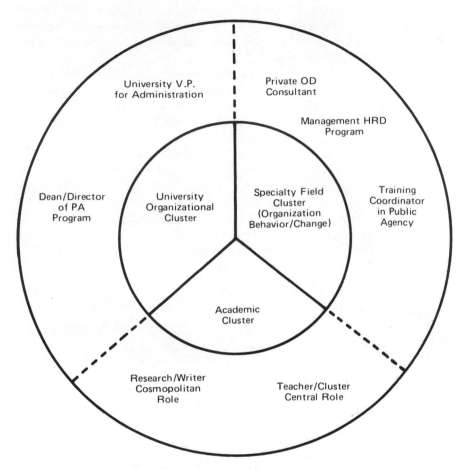

Figure 1 Sample career clusters/roles for PA academic.

and the increasingly in-career nature of the clientele suggests equal consideration of both perspectives. Faculty will need to be grounded in a philosophical
and theoretical base and have specialized practice-related skills as well. Such
an orientation suggests that those who have seen themselves primarily as having theory and scholarship orientations would be advised to seek practice opportunities either through consulting or longer assignments in a practice environment.

Attending to the practice context will clearly benefit the scholar/academic in his or her role as a public administration educator. Too often, the traditional scholar does not allow theoretical ideas to come up against a practice reality. Research projects can be enhanced in a practical context and will more effectively relate concepts to students. In the same way, the practitioner coming to the academic career role will benefit from the academic and ivory tower dimension of the university. The practitioner moving fresh from a role experience that emphasizes immediate practice issues will need the reflective refuge that the ivory tower provides. The scholar can place practice into a theoretical context. Perhaps the unique contribution of the theoretical side is to make sense of a particular practice method or approach in a new or unique way. The ivory tower thereby provides time for putting practice and skill into a conceptual frame.

In sum, the academic career requires people who can live in both worlds: practice and academic. Being effective in both settings enhances the career viability of the individual practitioner/educator and in turn improves the overall quality of public service education.

Notes

1. Mosher, F. C. *Democracy in the Public Service.* Oxford, New York, 1968.
2. The National Association of Schools of Public Affiars and Administration (NASPAA) is an organization whose member institutions represent schools offering degree programs in public administration and public affairs. Biennially, NASPAA issues a survey of activities by their member institutions. The information presented is derived principally from the surveys conducted since 1973.
3. National Association of Schools of Public Affiars/Public Administration, *Programs in Public Affairs and Public Administration, 1980.* Washington, D.C., 1980.
4. National Association of Schools of Public Affairs/Public Administration, *Programs in Public Affairs and Public Administration, 1978.* Washington, D.C., 1978.
5. National Association of Schools of Public Affairs/Public Administration, *Programs in Public Affairs and Public Administration, 1976.* Washington, D.C., 1976.
6. Morgan, R., Meier, K. J., Kearney, R. C., Hayes, S. W., and Birch, H. B., Reputation and Productivity Among U.S. Public Administration and Public Affairs Programs. *Public Administration Review 41*, 666–673 (1981).
7. Schein, E., *Career Dynamics.* Addison-Wesley, Reading, Mass., 1978.
8. Ibid.

Index

ANNALS OF PUBLIC ADMINISTRATION